LAWRENCE W. BOWKER

106 Robbins

Robbinsville, NJ

08691

(609) 259-5955

2 32 87573

Introduction to Data Security and Controls

Books and Training Products From QED

Database

Migrating to DB2
DB2: The Complete Guide to Implementation and Use
DB2 Design Review Guidelines
DB2: Maximizing Performance of Online Production Systems
Embedded SQL for DB2: Application Design and Programming
SQL for DB2 and SQL/DS Application Developers
Using DB2 to Build Decision Support Systems
The Data Dictionary: Concepts and Uses
Logical Data Base Design
Entity-Relationship Approach to Logical Data Base Design
Database Management Systems: Understanding and Applying Database Technology
Database Machines and Decision Support Systems: Third Wave Processing
IMS Design and Implementation Techniques
Repository Manager/MVS: Concepts, Facilities and Capabilities
How to Use ORACLE SQL*PLUS
ORACLE: Building High Performance Online Systems
ORACLE Design Review Guidelines
Using ORACLE to Build Decision Support Systems

Systems Engineering

Effective Methods of EDP Quality Assurance
Handbook of Screen Format Design
Managing Software Projects: Selecting and Using PC-Based Project Management Systems
The Complete Guide to Software Testing
A User's Guide for Defining Software Requirements
A Structured Approach to Systems Testing
Storyboard Prototyping: A New Approach to User Requirements Analysis
The Software Factory: Managing Software Development and Maintenance
Data Architecture: The Information Paradigm
Advanced Topics in Information Engineering
Software Engineering with Formal Software Metrics

Management

Introduction to Data Security and Control
CASE: The Potential and the Pitfalls

Management (cont'd)

Strategic and Operational Planning for Information Services
Information Systems Planning for Competitive Advantage
How to Automate Your Computer Center: Achieving Unattended Operations
Ethical Conflicts in Information and Computer Science, Technology, and Business
Mind Your Business: Managing the Impact of End-User Computing
Controlling the Future: Managing Technology-Driven Change

Data Communications

Data Communications: Concepts and Solutions
Designing and Implementing Ethernet Networks
Network Concepts and Architectures
Open Systems: The Guide to OSI and its Implementation

IBM Mainframe Series

QMF: How to Use Query Management Facility with DB2 and SQL/DS
DOS/VSE: Introduction to the Operating System
DOS/VSE: CICS Systems Programming
DOS/VSE/SP Guide for Systems Programming: Concepts, Programs, Macros, Subroutines
Advanced VSE System Programming Techniques
Systems Programmer's Problem Solver
VSAM: Guide to Optimization and Design
MVS/JCL: Mastering Job Control Language
MVS/TSO: Mastering CLISTS
MVS/TSO: Mastering Native Mode and ISPF
REXX in the TSO Environment

Video

DB2: Building Online Production Systems for Maximum Performance
Data Architecture: An Information Systems Strategy (Video)
Building Online Production Systems with ORACLE 6.0
Practical Data Modeling

Programming

C Language for Programmers
VAX/VMS: Mastering DCL Commands and Utilities

This is Only a Partial Listing. For Additional Information or a Free Catalog contact

QED Information Sciences, Inc. • P. O. Box 82-181 • Wellesley, MA 02181
Telephone: 800-343-4848 or 617-237-5656 or fax 617-235-0826

Introduction to Data Security and Controls

Second Edition

Edward R. Buck, III

QED Technical Publishing Group
Boston • Montreal • London

© 1991 QED Information Sciences, Inc.
P.O. Box 82-181
Wellesley, MA 02181

© 1991 Buck Data Security Consultants

Library of Congress Catalog Number: 91-12351
International Standard Book Number: 0-89435-383-7

Printed in the United States of America
91 92 93 10 9 8 7 6 5 4 3 2 1

Library of Congress Cataloging-in Publication Data
Buck, Edward R.
    Introduction to data security and controls / Edward R. Buck. —
2nd ed.
        p.   cm.
    Includes bibliographical references and index.
    ISBN 0-89435-383-7
    1.   Computers—Access control.   2. Electronic data processing
departments—Security measures.   I. Title.
QA76.9.A25B83   1991
005.8—dc20   91-12351
                                                                CIP

To My Sons, of whom I am very proud—
John, Christopher, and Michael

Contents

Preface

Computer or data security is a major problem in today's world of data processing. This book outlines the security problem, earlier perceptions, and present trends and issues. It also addresses current trends in security, communication networks, encryption, mini/micro technology, access licensing, user monitoring, and database management system characteristics.

The book is intended as an overview of data security and its rise to a current economic priority. Historically, management was ostrich-like in its approach to protection of information and equipment, believing that incidents of computer vulnerability were isolated, infrequent, and unlikely to happen. This attitude was reinforced by the added expense of security systems, which was viewed as disproportionate to potential losses.

Absolute security is impossible, but the perceptive DP professional will view the chronology of security breaches, and the extremely large loss potential, and hopefully conclude that the need for "insurance" is indeed real.

Top management was often aloof and uncomfortable in the EDP environment when the subject of computerization was too new and they lacked direct experience. The public was also leary of computerization, watching plastic money (tangible) turn into electronic money (intangible) and the quality of life become increasingly dependent on various types of data systems.

In addition, problems within the backup security plans were

beginning to surface. Methods were seldom based on the concept of "mission dependency." There was little prioritization of jobs to be run in an emergency and no analysis for cost-effectiveness. It was also difficult to justify the cost of hardware/software redundancy. Along with constant problems in updating emergency programs and master files, there were equipment incompatibilities between facilities.

American involvement in the Vietnam war, and its consequent protests, set up "the computer" as a symbol of establishment oppression. Civil disobedience produced direct attacks on many university and governmental systems, particularly if they were programmed for defense research. In the 1970s Dow Chemical had 1,000 tapes erased by protestors.

Attention now began to move from accidental to intentional security threats. However, the personnel involved in devising means of security control had little concept of any internal hostile danger.

Simplistic error identification and correction procedures were used. The internal system auditing procedures were rudimentary. Companies lost many millions of dollars annually due to a new problem of "white collar crime." These crimes, such as fraud, embezzlement, and espionage, were swept under the corporate carpet to avoid damaging publicity. Companies preferred to absorb the losses rather than expose their shortsightedness and areas of vulnerability.

One of the classic examples is the Equity Funding Corporation of America scandal, which was made public in 1973. Stanley Goldblum, chairman of the board, and others had succeeded in falsely inflating the value of company stock by selling bogus life insurance policies to other insurance companies. The policies were written for people who existed only in Equity's computer files.

The company actually had a special staff whose assignment was to alter or manufacture data on these nonexistent policyholders. The conspiracy continued for four years and might still be going on if it had not been reported by a former employee. The results were a $2.1 million fraud whose victims were the real Equity customers. The crime was not new, merely a variation on the old "money pyramid." The method, a surprisingly unsophisticated adulteration of a computer database, was finally being taken seriously. Also the discovery of inadequate auditing procedures was precedent to new required auditing procedures and legislation.

As white collar crime increased, investigation and prosecution lagged one step behind. Computer crime is clean and viewed as nonviolent. The perpetrator is often the intelligent but underpaid employee whose frustration with the fat cat corporation and unrecognized dedication are the necessary elements for a "get even" rationalization. Consequently, data security is very much a people problem, not only in terms of error or neglect but also in employee trustworthiness. Skilled DP professionals have the knowledge, access, and resources necessary to cripple the organization.

In 1972, careless disposal of proprietary information set the stage for theft by a person outside an organization. Jerry Neal Schneider, using discarded copies of operating guides and some self-designed investigative techniques, stole at least $1 million worth of electronic equipment from Pacific Telephone and Telegraph Company. After figuring out the access process, he ordered the equipment, from Western Electric, to be delivered to various public locations where he redeemed and resold it. He was charged with grand theft but served only forty days on a prison farm. The civil suit, instituted by Pacific Telephone for $250,000, was settled for $85,000. Schneider later sold his story to the movies and started working as a "security consultant."

In the 1980s came a new culprit on the computer scene, that being the hacker (i.e., person(s)) and the computer virus (code that attacks a system, reproduces, spreads, and disappears).

Distributed information systems and the networks that interconnect them have increasingly made corporations and government agencies targets of attack by perpetrators. The National Center for Computer Crime Data shows that banks and other commercial users of computer systems have been the prime targets of computer criminals. Of reported computer crimes in 1988, 36 percent were commercial users; 12 percent, banks; 17 percent, telecommunications; 17 percent, government; 12 percent, individuals; and 4 percent, universities. It also noted a higher than 10 percent increase in the areas of telecommunications and government installations compared to 1986.

In 1988, a former Cornell University graduate student, Robert T. Morris, made national news when he shut down thousands of computers with a virus program that spread itself throughout the Internet network. Commercial users, government, universities, and telecommunications sectors were all impacted by the computer crime.

As recent as March 1990, the Internet computer network was the victim of an unidentified hacker, who penetrated systems at Harvard University, Purdue University, and Digital Equipment Corporation. The nationwide network links research labs, universities, and other facilities. The hacker also accessed a work station of Sun Microsystems, Inc., at Los Alamos Laboratory and used it to access other systems on the network. He or she used the Los Alamos computer to run a decoding program on encrypted password files stolen from other systems.

This was not the first time Los Alamos had been struck by unauthorized access and use. In the mid-1980s, the FBI and New Mexico authorities raided a gambling establishment with a nationwide network and traced it back to Los Alamos Laboratory. They found gambling records and other information stored on the same disk packs as classified information dealing with nuclear research.

These are only a few of the well-known incidences of computer security violations resulting in crime. As management began to look at the cost (both in time and money) of unauthorized modification or existence without information, the scope of the problem became apparent. The average industrial downtime can cost between $1,000 and $100,000 a day. In addition, there is the expense of replacing hardware, software, and data files.

As computer systems are pushed out by end users, the responsibility for securing those systems is also distributed. That responsibility is not necessarily understood or readily accepted. The concept of anticipating threats and identifying vulnerabilities in a systematic way is a recent development. It has been conjectured that chronic lack of communication between users and DP professionals prevented serious use of "risk management" techniques (converting loss to dollar value). The user was the only one in a position to evaluate and quantify the organization's dependency on systems, whereas the DP professional was only able to attach value to hardware and software. The importance of a coherent management-level evaluation of data systems was not easy to recognize or put into practice.

Data security is based on two elements: first, security of a system is a problem which can be approached and dealt with through the same system analysis and design tools used for development of systems in general; second, the use of a management science methodology, called risk management, is needed for informed decision making on the potential loss value of security risks and the potential effectiveness of security countermeasures.

Computer systems have been created to deal with complexity, which can also include designed-in complex security measures. In effect, computer technology itself is the best (and in most cases, the only) means of protecting computer resources of all types from attack.

In protecting computer resources, the use of computer technology is the most effective data security tool available. Hardware and software can be designed in ways to make data safe from both intentional and unintentional threats. Total computer security is never possible, but the computer can execute controls that are so complex as to make the cost of system penetration prohibitive.

Presentation to management of the risk analysis team's conclusions must inspire confidence and demonstrate the professionalism of the team. No matter how good the risk analysis is, if management's perception of it is poor, then overall the system, or possibly the corporation, is likely to suffer.

Computers and the information they process and contain should be considered property and, like any other property, should be protected from damage, loss, disclosure, alteration, and stealing.

In conclusion, I am confident that the decade of the 1990s—for all its rigors—will stimulate the data processing profession to new levels of technological accomplishment and new levels of service to the nation, with increased levels of protection from the vulnerabilities resulting from increased complexity of our systems.

Edward "Sandy" Buck
Hampton Beach, New Hampshire

Data Security Policy Statement Example

A data security policy ensures that all information existing in computerized form by properly safeguarded; and that the computer processes involved in the collection, creation, manipulation, storage, retrieval, transmission, and display of such information be similarly safeguarded, both in a manner appropriate to its value to the company and its potential for loss or unauthorized disclosure.

Personnel responsible for the administration of data security safeguards shall provide for and ensure the safeguarding of information and computer processes. Safeguards appropriate to contractual requirements for information and computer processes employed within computer technology control shall be implemented where applicable.

The foregoing statement of policy shall be communicated to employees, and procedures essential for implementation of the policy shall be instituted.

Cartoon reprinted with permission of Field Enterprises, Inc.

Introduction

The information presented here will identify the general context of data security, including the need for security and the reasons why earlier approaches are no longer sufficient. The reader will gain a basic appreciation for some of the new methods for dealing with data security, along with an exposure to the terminology of these methods.

This book is designed to familiarize the reader with the need for data security and the basic methods used to provide good security. One recurrent theme is that security is everybody's business, regardless of functional role performed. Another major theme is that modern computer systems, being so complex, offer many avenues for attack by intentional or unintentional threat agents. The computer system has been created to deal with complexity, which can also include designed-in complex security measures. In effect, computer technology itself is the best (and in many cases, the only) means of protecting computer resources of all types from attack.

The need for data security has always been present to some degree since the advent of the most rudimentary data processing techniques. Data and the procedures and equipment used to manipulate it have always had some value in themselves. The important difference in the modern era of automation is that individuals, corporations, and governments are becoming increasingly dependent upon these resources for their operation and even existence. Additionally, the problem of crime by use of computer-associated techniques has increased greatly because of the common vulnerability of the data in the system to manipulation or copying without a trace of evidence. Even more important in some ways is the fact that computer systems frequently contain large amounts of sensitive information about people, company proprietary activities, and national secrets which must be protected from improper use and disclosure.

This module of instruction is intended to introduce the reader to these problems, so that he/she will develop basic security awareness. Some of the traditional and less effective solutions will be discussed with their shortcomings identified. The newer methods of data security will be briefly introduced for later development. This modern concept of data security is based on two elements: first, security of a system is a problem which can be approached and dealt with by use of the same system analysis and design tools used for development of systems in general; second, the use of a management science methodology called risk management is needed for informed decision making on the potential loss value of security risks and the potential effectiveness of security countermeasures.

TOPIC 1   WHY DATA SECURITY? THE PROBLEM STATEMENT

In this section, the basic statement of the data security problem will be developed. For comparison purposes, the evolution of computer dependency will be discussed, showing why early approaches to data security are no longer adequate.

I. Earlier Perception of the Problem

Prior to 1960, data processing was generally used to replace or augment general clerical or accounting functions. There was no basic dependency on these systems of punch-card tabulation, mainly because of their slowness and frequent unreliability. Following the business computer's introduction, the same general philosophy of automation utility was common.

At that time, computers were not critical to business and security. Few applications were automated; business pace was slower; and backup manual systems were common. In addition, there was a strong resistance to automation in many sectors of business. Equipment costs were high. There was almost no private ownership of equipment, and an equipment investment needed major protection.

The technology was esoteric. Few understood the operation of computers or knew how to program with the rudimentary programming languages. Application sophistication was low. The manual review of I/O was common, and updates were batch oriented.

There was little danger of sophisticated fraud schemes, and little perceived threat from international agents. With the high cost of equipment, media, and supplies, protection of resources from natural disaster became the primary concern.

II. Present and Future Scope of Problem

The problem of security has changed. Computers and data resources are becoming increasingly embedded in the texture of business and society. Furthermore, very sophisticated EDP knowledge and equipment is now commonly available for private individuals to exploit.

As society is dependent on computers for basic functions, failure or serious disruption of computer systems would be expensive or actually dangerous to human life in many cases. Vital areas which must be protected include:

1. Building environmental systems
2. Life support systems in medical centers
3. Air traffic control
4. Mass transit systems
5. Traffic signals
6. Telephone systems
7. Support payments to individuals
   a. Social Security
   b. Welfare and Social Aid
   c. Unemployment compensation
   d. Most government and corporate payrolls

Modern business is similarly dependent. Its operations are so centered on the computer system that protection of business requires protection of its computer systems. Businesses can fail if the accounts receivable data is lost.

Let's examine the characteristics of modern business which demands security of its computer system.

First of all, most businesses now have a complete dependency on automated functions. These include automated customer billing, payroll, accounting, marketing, production, and inventory control. In addition, because the tempo of business requires rapid processing, modern business systems must be highly responsive and inherently reliable. In many cases, a few hours of downtime can be disastrous, even when data recovery is complete. This is because plants and offices are interconnected. There is a meshing of diverse business functions with certain functions such as marketing, personnel, and financial management highly interdependent in many cases. In addition, customer lists and order processing, as well as reservations for services such as transportation and lodging, are definitely impacted by downtime.

Because manual backups are in some cases virtually impossible with modern systems, it has become increasingly necessary to accept total dependency on the operating automated system. Manual backups are not practical as systems are often too complex, manual methods are not responsive enough, and backup is not viewed as cost effective.

On the other hand, the cost benefit of protective countermeasures is rapidly improving. While the value of data resources has greatly increased, the cost of some countermeasures has declined.

Let us now consider the factors presently increasing which demand serious consideration of security measures.

Social pressure and laws to control computers and data are on the increase. The public is concerned with privacy issues such as the ease of unauthorized access and collection of personal data, combining databases to expand data on individuals, and the potential for misuse of this data.

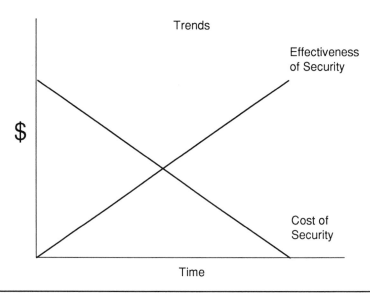

Figure 1.1. Cost benefit of security.

With increased emphasis on consumerism, poor implementation of automated systems that affect the public has caused growing distrust and animosity. Consumer efforts are leading to ENFORCED regulation. The integrity of these systems must be unquestioned. Thus, concerns are the point of sale (POS) systems and price markings (UID bar codes); billing systems; and loss of the human element.

Regulations on auditability of automated systems are the natural outgrowth of all this. Considerations here are:

1. Foreign and Corrupt Practices Act.
2. No hard copy records of transactions.
3. IRS pending audit regulations.
4. Requirements for documentation of system operations. Auditing firms are pressing for required standards on system operation and documentation.

For many reasons, the threat to computer resources has sharply increased. Because of widespread digital communications, network reliability is not yet common; computers can be accessed from many locations, and systems are vulnerable to tapping or disruption.

Sophisticated personal computers have become available to everyone at low cost, with the potential for illegal entry to systems.

The understanding of computer technology is rapidly spreading. It is no longer esoteric; high school students can now penetrate systems.

For many reasons, sophisticated terrorism/sabotage can be expected to increase. For example, dependency on computer systems is common knowledge, which means a high potential for disruption. There have been sabotage incidents at computer centers, and it is generally acknowledged that disgruntled workers can wreak havoc.

The fact that computer systems have increased in complexity is itself a problem, making more openings for attack. As few understand the complete workings of large systems, security measures must be proportionally complex.

III. Basic Statement of the Problem

A. The Systems Security Problem:

1. Systems are increasingly vulnerable to disruption.
2. There are increased threats.
3. Methods are needed to "cope."

B. Overall Guiding Principles of Security Enhancement:

   1. "The level of dependency of an organization upon its information processing resources specifies the basic degree of protection needed."

     a. Requires careful assessment of dependency.

     b. Requires the assignment of value to this dependency.

     c. Requires the identification of potential threats to this dependency.

   2. "The value of the resources to others determines additional protection needed."

     a. Estimation of fraud potential.

     b. Estimation of loss (data or other) potential.

     c. Nature of proprietary information in system.

     d. Nature of other entrusted information (e.g., national security) in systems.

   3. "Barriers of protection must be erected to the extent that they are less expensive than the cost of possible loss."

     a. Kinds of potential loss.

     b. Value of potential loss by type.

     c. Possible barriers to loss and their cost.

   4. "Barriers must be multi-dimensional to cover all significant threats."

     a. Different categories of threats possible.

     b. Various levels of barrier sophistication.

     c. Layers of barriers of different types needed.

IV. Topic Review

   1. List some key factors which form the requirement for better data security.

   2. Describe some problems associated with traditional approaches to data security.

   3. Review significant trends and promising developments in solving data security problems.

TOPIC 2   TRADITIONAL APPROACHES TO DATA SECURITY

I. Physical Security Emphasis

The original approach to data security, and its predominant concern, was in terms of physical security. This meant protection of the

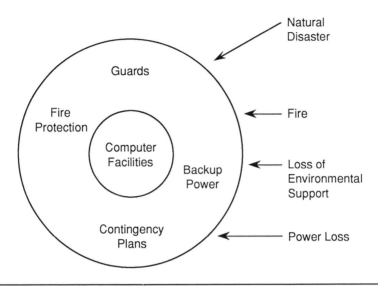

Figure 1.2. Early approach view of systems security.

equipment, programs, and data from damage or destruction by inadvertent means such as natural disaster or human error. The objects requiring physical security were:

1. Physical plant where computer resources were located
2. Environmental support equipment
3. Computer hardware
4. Programs: documentation, media
5. Data files: source documents, media

At this time the cost of hardware was the initial driving factor, as it was proportionally very high in the early years and easy to quantify and deal with. There was no perception of the threat from hostile agents, and corporate pride in owning a computer was reflected with computer rooms as public showplaces. Natural or environmental disaster was the only major perceived threat.

Because of this environment, emergency measures were planned to cope with natural disasters such as flood, earthquake, tornadoes, and hurricanes. Fire and water damage as well as electrical outages were of concern. In the immediate support area, failure of the air conditioning/heating and the water supply for equipment cooling posed a continual threat.

II. Emergency Backup for Continuity of Operations

During this period the concepts of emergency backup programs consisted of on-site duplication, such as additional hardware components, generators for electrical supply, air conditioning components, and generations of file tape. Off-site alternatives consisted of backup agreements with other DP facilities and storage of programs and master files.

There were several problems with these backup security plans. These methods were seldom clearly based on the concept of mission dependency. There was little prioritization of jobs to be run in an emergency and no analysis for cost-effectiveness. At the same time it was difficult to cost-justify hardware/software redundancy. Along with constant problems in maintaining currency of emergency programs and master files, there were equipment incompatibilities between facilities.

III. Rudimentary Personnel and Procedural Controls

The personnel involved in devising means of security control had little concept of any internal hostile threat. Simplistic error identification and correction procedures were used. The internal system auditing procedures were rudimentary.

IV. No Comprehensive Risk Management Programs

The concept of anticipating threats and identifying system vulnerabilities in a systematic way is a recent development. It has been conjectured that chronic lack of communication between users and DP professionals prevented serious use of risk management techniques. The user alone was in a position to evaluate and quantify organization dependency on systems. The DP professional was only able to attach value to hardware and software. The importance of a coherent management level evaluation of data systems was not easy to recognize or put into practice.

V. "Amulet Security"

When security of data systems became a serious concern in the late sixties, numerous wrong turns were made. This can largely be attributed to lack of serious research in the area of security. Computer scientists have only recently begun to realize the importance of serious data security research. One wrong turn has been called "Amulet Security," after the medieval practice of wearing a magical charm to ward off danger or sickness. This sensationalist approach has taken the form, for example, of installing magnet detectors in tape libraries when it was thought that small magnets could be used to rapidly sabotage tapes. The result of this intuitive approach has been "costly solutions to nonexistent security threats or ineffective solutions to real threats" (Jacobson, 76).

VI. *"Thirty Year Law"*

This law has been humorously proposed to account for the human tendency to deal rationally only with things that we have directly experienced (Jacobson, 76). "It has never happened here, therefore it can't happen," is another way of expressing the same trait. A corollary to this law, proposed by the author, is that "it can happen to you, but it can't happen to me." This is a problem that the data security administrator or system developer will face in attempting to obtain management approval for installation of expensive security countermeasures. The only way of combatting this attitude is by conducting a carefully documented risk analysis.

VII. *Topic Review*

1. State the principal components of the early emphasis on physical security and their limitations.
2. Describe the types of measures commonly used in the past for continuity of operations under emergency conditions and the limitations of these measures.
3. Recognize the common nature of personnel and procedural controls used until recently and their limitations.
4. Recall the major reasons for the absence of comprehensive corporate data security risk management programs.
5. Recall the erroneous approach to data security represented by the term "Amulet Security."
6. Recall the managerial perceptual problems typified by the concept of the "Thirty Year Law."

TOPIC 3   TRENDS AND PRIORITIES IN PROBLEM SOLUTION

I. *Impact of New Hardware Technology*

Computer hardware technology has advanced more rapidly than any other component of the industry. Several new developments can be

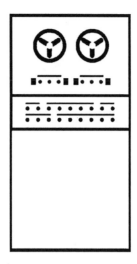

used effectively for data security purposes. For example, the communications networks have improved, meaning there is greater internal reliability along with many built-in security features. Also, the Federal Data Encryption Standard (DES) has been developed for broad private and public use. DES modules are now available on LSI chips at relatively low cost. Encryption is one of the surest means of implementing data security. Encryption of stored data and of all communication links with the CPU is now feasible. Mini and microprocessor technology has made possible the pre-editing of data, as well as security monitors for mainframes, access controllers, and other system control applications.

II. Software Technology

Installing very high security in systems software is a formidable task. Most of the current security research has been concentrated in this area. The major problem is that ingenious programmers are often able to take control of the operating system and thereby defeat most other security measures that have been implemented.

Security measures to protect the operating systems must be implemented in areas of securing kernels, virtual machine monitors (VMM), and memory protection.

For the security-oriented DBMS, data integrity must be emphasized with the considerations of reconstructability and auditability. The database must be protected and kept private through user identifiability, access licensing to data element level, defining usage privileges, and monitoring user activities.

III. Recognition of Data Security as a Systems Problem

Data security is a basic and necessary function of any system. The overall set of functions to be performed by a system includes protection of assets which may become exposed in connection with processing.

Security requirements are functional system design requirements. For example, to assure data integrity and reliability, accuracy of the database as well as recoverability and re-creatability are essential. In addition, data access restriction must be sensitive, of intrinsic value, company dependent, and required to be known.

New system design conceptual tools can identify and formulate data system security requirements. These tools are:

1. Structured analysis
2. Functional decomposition
3. Egoless programming
4. Structured walkthroughs

IV. Risk Management Approach

The risk management approach is a formal one. It is based on a set of methods from management science, and its purpose is to deal with data security in a rigorous and coherent way.

Risk management is intended to involve management through surfacing data security as a major corporate concern. This concern is then expressed by formulating straightforward business decisions. These decisions consider the level of risk to be tolerated in dollars, the cost of protection alternatives in dollars, and trade-offs.

The complexity and technical nature of data security do not fit well into traditional industrial security organizations. A separate data security administration is required, having the following functions:

1. Corporate level security risk analysis
2. Policy and standards for data security
3. Monitoring of data security
4. Security education

Risk analysis methodology, which is the core of the risk analysis approach, is a formal procedure to analyze threats and system vulnerabilities and then to express them in quantitative terms of probabilities and anticipated loss. A separate section of this book will cover this subject in more detail.

In protecting computer resources, the use of computer technology is the most effective data security tool available. Hardware and software can be designed in ways to make data safe from both intentional and unintentional threats.

Complete security is never possible, but the computer can execute controls that are so complex as to make the cost of system penetration prohibitive.

V. Topic Review

1. List the ways new computer hardware technology can impact the data security problem.
2. Describe what areas of new software technology should be controlled by data security measures.
3. Recall that data security requirements can be identified and formulated in the same manner as other functional system design requirements by the use of new conceptual tools for design.
4. Review the basic elements of the risk management approach to data security.

2

Total Risk Management—
The Data Security
Program

In the last few years, major corporations and Government agencies have recognized the need for formal data security programs. The security of corporate data systems assets has become such an important issue that it can no longer be left to piecemeal implementation by concerned system designers and operations personnel. Nor can the technical aspects of data security be effectively managed by traditional industrial security methods.

This chapter presents a growing industry-wide approach to total risk management via corporate data security programs. The general requirements for a program of this nature in any corporation are developed in terms of program objectives, organizational structure, and general functions to be performed.

In our first topic we shall examine the need for corporate security programs, as well as the objectives of such programs and their organization.

The second topic deals with policy on the categorization of system data according to a set of sensitivity attributes which the data may possess. These attributes form the basic judgmental criteria upon which selection of protective security countermeasures for the data are based.

TOPIC 1 WHY A CORPORATE DATA SECURITY PROGRAM IS NEEDED

Introduction

This module develops the rationale for a corporate data security program. Data security is not well suited to traditional industrial security management due to its highly technical nature and the level of sophistication required.

A. Growing corporate dependence on computer systems.

Major business functions are automated.
Few systems permit alternative manual processing.

B. Special problems in securing computer systems.

Systems are highly complex and become less understood as they evolve.
Many avenues of attack are possible.
Concentric layers of security are needed.

C. Internal and external value of computer system resources.

1. Internal value
   Cost of hardware and plant
   Development cost of application software
   Time-value of operational systems processing
   Resource-value of data in operational systems
2. External value
   Value of access to unauthorized persons
   Value of data held in trust for others

I. Objectives of a Data Security Program

A data security program is designed to overcome these problems and adequately protect the corporate data systems assets.

A. Achieve the most effective and economic corporate data security posture.

Perform risk analyses to identify loss potential.
Implement countermeasures which provide protection needed at lower cost.

B. Set policy and standards.

The nature of data security requires the use of standard security practices in all application systems.

Basic security policy for general corporate hardware and software use needs to be set.

C. Identify data security problems and requirements.

Monitor systems and procedures.

Test system controls for a weaknesses.

D. Obtain adequate data security resources.

Corporate risk analysis to identify broad needs.

Monitor budgeting processes to determine if security expenses are adequate to meet needs.

II. Data Security Organization

An aggressive data security program requires an organizational structure with the strength to carry out the program objectives.

A. Data security organization in a company requires establishment of a hierarchy of clearly defined security responsibilities.

B. The data security administrator requires adequate authority to do the job. This implies organizational independence from data systems and users.

III. Topic Review

1. Recall three main reasons why a corporate data security program is needed.
2. List four key objectives to be attained by a corporate data security program.
3. Recall the three main organizational criteria required in establishing a corporate data security administrative organization.
4. Review six important functions that should be performed by the corporate data security administrative organization.

TOPIC 2   VOCABULARY OF THE APPROACH

This data security book uses several highly specialized terms that must be defined for the reader. In addition, several basic security functions and principles are explained. Therefore, certain definitions are presented here so that the reader will have a general familiarity with the terms used later in the book where precise definitions and examples will be discussed.

I. Basic Terms

A. Security

The protection of data system resources against accidental or intentional destruction, disclosure, modification. Computer security refers to technological safeguards and managerial procedures which can be applied to system resources to protect organizational assets and individual privacy. In this book the word security is often used to encompass three other important ideas taken together:

Protection
Integrity
Reliability

B. Protection

Defense or safeguard against attack by some intentional or unintentional threat agent.

C. Integrity

Completeness and accuracy of data, either as separate elements or in consistency of relationship among elements. Includes the concept of continued data existence and recoverability from error.

D. Reliability

Dependability of a system to perform exactly as expected, without error.

E. Privacy

Relating to information about a person and, specifically, the rights of an individual to restrict access or dissemination of information about himself or herself.

F. Countermeasures

Methods of any type (e.g., physical, procedural, hardware, software, personnel) employed to counteract a threat to the system.

G. Controls

Generally identical to countermeasures, as used in this book. Methods used to regulate the system so that it performs according to specified criteria.

H. Access

This term relates to gaining admittance in any way to data or making use of any resource in a computer system. It specifically refers to a set of protective countermeasures against unauthorized admittance to or disclosure of data.

I. Usage

This term relates to the integrity of data. It specifically refers to a set of protective countermeasures to assure and maintain validity of data and to provide for its continued existence and recoverability.

II. Risk Management Terms

A. Threat

An aspect of the systems environment that, if given an opportunity, could cause harm to the organization.

B. Threat Agent

The means by which a threat materializes.

C. Vulnerability

Any weakness or flaw existing in a system. More specifically, the susceptibility of a system to a specific threat attack, or the opportunity available to a threat agent to mount that attack. A vulnerability in a system may exist independently of any known or probable threat.

D. Exposure

Exposure is the degree of relative availability of data in the environment in which it is used. In this sense, data exposure is one major aspect of system vulnerability. Access and usage (see above) are the two major categories of exposure.

E. Loss

To be deprived of a thing of value. As used in risk management, loss is the quantitative measure of expected deprivation due to a threat acting upon a vulnerable system resource.

F. Risk

The probability or likelihood that a threat agent will successfully mount a specific attack against a particular system vulnerability.

G. Risk Analysis

A method of analyzing system assets and vulnerabilities to establish an expected loss from threats based upon probabilities of occurrence. The object of risk analysis is to assess the degree of acceptability of each risk to system operation.

III. Some Basic Security Functions

A. Identity Authentication

Identity authentication refers to a set of manual or automated procedures which verify that a user requesting access is who he/she claims to be.

B. Access Authorization

Permission granted to an object (person, terminal, program) to perform a set of operations in the system. Access authorization is normally expressed in terms of a profile matrix which gives access privileges in terms of users, terminals, programs, data elements, type of access (e.g., read, write), and time period when operations are permitted.

C. Logging

A record that is kept either manually or by the computer system to keep track of events which take place with respect to the system.

D. Journaling

An in-depth form of logging in which all significant access or file activity events are recorded in their entirety. A complete journal would have a record, for example, of all data elements accessed by a user, the old and new images of any data changed, any images added or deleted, and the like. Using earlier copies of a file plus a journal, it would be possible to reconstruct the file at any point and identify the ways it has changed over a period of time.

IV. Security Design Principles

A. Objectives of Defense

All security defensive measures are intended to satisfy one or more of the following objectives:

Prevent occurrence of the exposure by erecting barriers between any threat and the vulnerabilities to it.

Minimize or contain the impact of any damage, mainly through the use of successive layers of protection so that a threat agent is restricted in what it can do.

Maximize recovery from the damage. Provide for ways of circumventing the damage, such as by the use of backup and reconstruction of files.

B. Default to Denial of Access

Design the system so that access authorizations are mandatory and those without the authorization are locked out.

C. Nonsecret Design

If bright people are given free opportunity to examine the system under development, they should be able to find security holes overlooked by the designers. For example, a modern principle of cryptography is that it is expected that the enemy may know how the system works, but is still prohibited from access to the system because he/she cannot obtain the necessary keys or enabling parameters.

D. User Acceptability

If the security provisions of a system are not user-engineered, then users will find ways (often nonsecure) of bypassing the system.

E. Complete Mediation of Accesses

The system should be designed so that all attempts to access the system or data are checked for levels of authorization privilege before access is granted.

F. Least Privilege

Refers to the access profile matrix in which each user, terminal, program, and type of data element may be given a separate access sensitivity license. For any combination of these factors, the lowest privilege of access of any of the factors will govern the access license for the whole combination.

G. Economy of Mechanism

The security design should be kept as small and simple as possible. The more complex any system is, the greater the number of potential errors.

H Separation of Privilege

For highly sensitive systems or data, the access authorization should require more than one privileged object. As an example, gaining access to the access authorization matrix in order to change levels should require the formal collaboration of two trusted employees, each knowing only part of the procedure or access parameters.

I. Least Common Mechanism

More than one program or user should not share file work areas, for example, because this could be an exploitable data path.

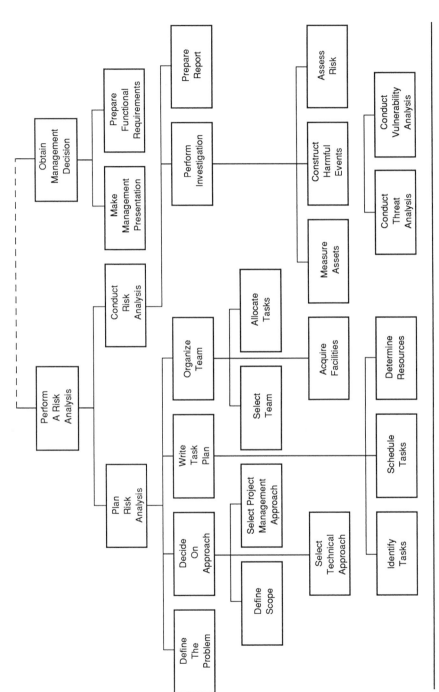

Figure 2.1. Risk analysis function model.

V. Topic Review

1. Recognize the nine basic data security terms used in the course.
2. Review the seven specific risk management terms used in the course.
3. Recall the four basic security functions which would normally be performed by the computer system.
4. Recognize the implications of nine basic security design principles to be discussed in the course.

3

An Introduction to
Risk Analysis

Uncertain events must be accounted for by data processing management to ensure that the organization mission is not interfered with. Management must know about the kinds of events that could happen, the vulnerability of the mission to an occurrence of one of those events, and the overall uncertainty faced by the mission operating in the threat environment. When these things are known, steps can be taken to anticipate occurrences of uncertain events and minimize their harmful effects. Attention to this management responsibility has become both more important and more difficult as computers take over vital mission functions.

TOPIC 1   CONCEPTS OF RISK ANALYSIS

An overall methodology for addressing the problem has begun to evolve in a disciplined form. This methodology is called risk management. Risk management, then, deals with identification, measurement, and control of uncertain events. The first element of risk management, identification and measurement, is called risk analysis and is the subject of this unit. The material under this topic will address the concept of risk analysis, its purpose, and methods for using the information gathered by a risk analysis project. As the details of how a risk analysis project is organized and executed are beyond the scope of this book, we will concentrate on how the results of risk analysis impact upon the systems development process.

A viable security program recognizes the potential for losses related to automated systems; therefore, management at all corporate levels must be involved in risk management. With this involvement, some problems emerge:

- Security procedures are costly. They often involve trade-offs in the areas of profits, user convenience, and speed of service.
- Complete security of computer systems is generally impossible. Therefore, management must decide on "acceptable levels of risk."
- There are many aspects of an automated system, from its database to its application software, that are subject to risks.
- The hazards involved take many forms. Some are obvious and well known, while others may be obscure.

The basic purpose of risk management is to have controlled and knowledgeable decision-making in regard to the protection of valuable and complex corporate resources. Therefore, risk management is accountable for:

Identifying risks
Measuring the likelihood and impact of loss
Controlling risks by instituting countermeasures

In order for risk management to be most effective, data processing managers and the functional users of automated systems must become aware of it and be actively engaged in its support.

Topic Review

1. Recall the purpose and principles of the risk analysis procedure.
2. Understand the areas of responsibility in risk management.

TOPIC 2   RISK ANALYSIS PURPOSE AND PRINCIPLES

Introduction

The primary purpose of performing a risk analysis is to advise corporate managers of the potential losses that could occur from intentional or accidental events. Therefore, the risk analysis is one component of a larger corporate management function—risk management. This task deals with the risk management function and the ways in which performing a risk analysis contributes to the overall corporate security program. Good risk analysis is the keystone of an effective risk management program. It provides a basis for making risk management decisions.

In this topic, you will learn the major elements of a risk management program and see how the risk analysis fits into the bigger picture. Objectives of the risk analysis and some standards of excellence are presented in order to provide you with the management philosophy of the risk analysis. In the following topics, the concepts and procedures of risk analysis will be developed upon the management aspects presented here.

I. The Risk Management Model

A. Definition of Risk Management

"An element of management science that is concerned with the identification, measurement, and control of uncertain events."

This definition of risk management is general in nature but states the problem well. Risk management is a management problem and concerns the enterprise as a whole. The management responsibility to ensure performance of the enterprise's mission is threatened by the possibility of uncertain events ranging from natural disaster, to vandalism, to sophisticated attempts to commit fraud. The task of identifying and understanding these threats, and then doing something about them, is what risk management is about.

The magnitude of the risk management problem is imposing. The systems to be protected are so complex and threatened by so many potential sources of harm that it is impossible to address every potential problem. Therefore, an orderly approach to dealing with the problem is needed.

B. Functions of Risk Management

The risk management function covers the entire security spectrum from initial identification of risk potential to implementation of safeguards to protect the system assets. Figure 3.1 shows the functions of risk management.

1. Risk analysis

Risk analysis is a systematic investigation of an environment to discover threat potential and then quantify the impact of that potential on the organization. Risk analysis is performed as a project using a specialized

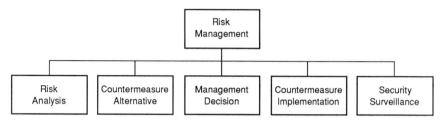

Figure 3.1. Functions of risk management.

team of people and disciplined investigative tools. The results produced are a statement of what risk situations exist as well as the potential for harm from them. If properly done, this statement can be used to generate a series of functional requirements for security protection.

2. Countermeasure alternative design

With a set of security requirements defined, it is possible to design a set of defenses that can be implemented to satisfy those requirements. Typically, a number of alternative defenses, or countermeasures, are formulated in order to give management a choice of how to respond to the risk situation.

3. Management decision

A critical part of the risk management "process" is the direct involvement of company management in the countermeasure implementation decision. The question of which risks can be tolerated and which must be responded to is complex and must be made in consideration of corporate goals, budget constraints, and so on.

4. Countermeasure implementation

With properly designed countermeasures, the implementation task is highly similar to more familiar systems implementations.

5. Security surveillance

After countermeasures are installed, they must be monitored for continued effectiveness. Additionally, the risk environment must be constantly evaluated to ensure that the defense elements of the system do not become obsolete.

II. Risk Analysis as a Risk Management Component

Risk analysis has become a specialized discipline of its own. It is a formidable task to look at all aspects of data processing activity to assure that all sources of harm have been considered. A data processing activity typically includes complex manual operations, large numbers of people, diverse types of hardware, and external communications facilities. The potential sources of harm are endless, including such things as power loss, disgruntled employees, vandals, human errors, machine failures, and so on,.

Several methodologies have been devised to provide a systematic approach to the problem. Almost all of these are based on quantifying the probability of occurrence of harmful events, quantifying the loss to be sustained by an occurrence, and calculating an annual loss expectancy (ALE). When dollar figures can be attached to the threatening elements of the data processing environment, it is possible to make straightforward decisions about which risks deserve greatest attention and how much it is practical to spend when responding to the various identified threats. Many of the formal methodologies are quite elaborate, involving extensive probability calculations and sophisticated reporting techniques. The end result of applications of these approaches (risk analysis models) is simply a list of risk elements and a statement of their importance.

The output of the risk analysis is carried forward in the risk management model (See Figure 3.2) to provide the basis for counter-measure design. Note that this activity takes place at the corporate

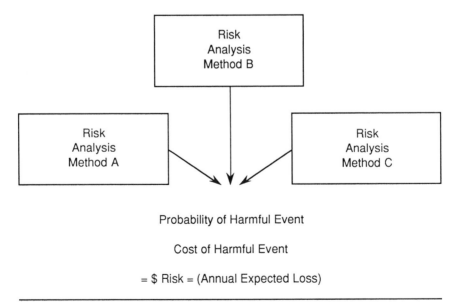

Probability of Harmful Event

Cost of Harmful Event

= $ Risk = (Annual Expected Loss)

Figure 3.2. Risk analysis models.

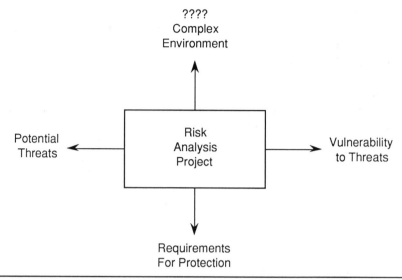

Figure 3.3. Areas of risk analysis information.

level crossing the boundaries of individual data systems. The results of the risk analysis must be understood by system designers responsible for generating countermeasure design alternatives.

The results are important in another context, however. A new data system design must consider the requirements for protection that are implied by the corporate risk analysis results. Individual applications systems must frequently contain their own protection features as an integral part of the system design.

A. Objectives of Risk Analysis

1. Provide a systematic approach to identifying and measuring sources of potential harm.
2. Produce a rational set of guidelines for design of counter-measures.
3. Prepare information adequate to support management decision.

B. Criteria for Successful Risk Analysis

1. Comprehensive

The risk analysis results should ideally account for every source of potential harm. An even more demanding requirement is that the methodology used should itself demonstrate to the reader how completeness has been obtained.

2. *Understandable*

The risk analysis results are intended to serve as input to management decision and the countermeasure design process. Documentation, therefore, must be produced in terms that relate to these dissimilar audiences. Given the technical nature of many of the risk considerations, appropriate reporting can be difficult.

3. *Technically sound*

Risk analysis is a multi-disciplinary task. In-depth investigation of many diverse technical areas in the data processing activity must be performed. This requires detailed input from such diverse disciplines as personnel management and computer system hardware maintenance.

C. Components of Risk Analysis

Risk analysis is a quantitative measure of the potential for losses resulting from occurrences of uncertain events in some time period. The task of risk analysis is to calculate and report that expected loss at a detailed level. A loss occurs when a threatening agent acts upon a system asset in some harmful way. The threatening agent acts on the asset as the result of some opportunity. That opportunity is called the

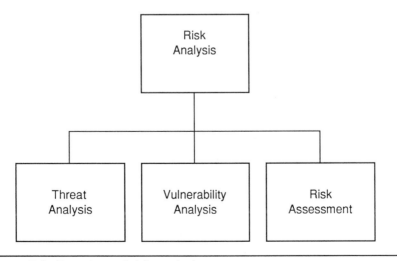

Figure 3.4. Functions of risk analysis.

vulnerability and must be accounted for in trying to assess the risk level. Essential elements contributing to the level of risk are: threat, vulnerability, and impact on assets. The major functions of risk analysis shown in Figure 3.4 are aimed at quantifying these risk components:

1. Threat analysis
2. Vulnerability analysis
3. Risk assessment

D. Past Approaches to Risk Analysis

Traditional approaches to risk management have employed a variety of risk analysis methods, which generally have these common considerations:

Likelihood of a harmful event
Cost of the harmful event

Tradition has shown that management should institute counter-measures that cost less than the expected loss. Therefore, management has instituted countermeasures to control risk at some "acceptable level."

Most of the traditional approaches to risk management have been oriented to losses resulting from natural disasters and accidents. The outcomes of an aggressively conducted risk management program do not eliminate hazards. However, as a minimum, these hazards have been identified and evaluated.

In the past, managers have provided these general criticisms of risk analyses:

1. Current methods are very labor intensive and take valuable workers away from their principal jobs.
2. Results of risk analysis do not relate realistically to the work-day environment.
3. Risk analysis results are not stated in terms pertinent to the management decision process.

III. Implementation of Risk Analysis

To be successful, data processing personnel, users, and security managers must all become involved in the planning, in-progress reviews, and results of the risk analysis. Initially, concentration should be on the major assets and threats; a concept of the "big picture" is essential before becoming immersed in details. In other words, an emphasis should not be placed on collecting estimates or data that are overly precise. Avoid dissipating the team's energy and interest by listing all data items in the database. This could become necessary at a later time (hopefully not!), but initially evaluate the major aspects of the security environment. Natural disasters and accidents may be easier to analyze; however, malice, fraud, and ineptness can produce high impact losses.

While conducting the risk analysis, it is important to remember that the format and content of the analysis may change depending on the level at which it is conducted (i.e., entire corporation versus single application). Regardless of the level, however, the risk analysis should adhere to a set of common concepts and procedures. A systematic approach contributes most to a comprehensive product.

A top-down approach to planning and conducting the risk analysis is most effective and is recommended for the following reasons:

1. It provides for the best use of team member's time.
2. It contributes to a regimented approach.

In considering the objectives of the risk analysis, it should be emphasized that a good risk analysis transforms the very complex security environment from the user's data processor's perspective into quantified threats and requirements. From this compiled set of harmful events, each potentially hazardous event will be considered in terms of its likelihood and impact. The conclusions must provide a reasonable and logical basis for establishing countermeasures.

Most importantly, management should be able to *use* and *understand* the results of the risk analysis for the following reasons:

Managers use risk analysis to make decisions in the risk management model, to buy insurance, and to formulate corporate plans.

The *Data Security Administrator* uses the analysis as a keystone of requirements definition and security program.

The *designer* of a system uses the risk analysis as a basis for writing functional requirements for the system.

In judging a risk analysis, the following criteria or standards should be considered:

1. The results are based on a complete and systematic analysis.
2. The analysis is understandable to a group of multi-level users.
3. The analysis employs correct techniques and logical procedures.

IV. Summary

In reviewing the material presented so far, we come to the following conclusions:

1. A rigorous and visible risk management program is a necessity for any modern corporate security program.
2. A risk management model aids in specifying the elements of the risk management program.
3. The risk management model shown here is applicable to multiple levels of an organization and can be applied to a system, a data center, or a corporate security program.
4. Successive replications of the model serve to refine the procedures and allow more detail.

V. Topic Review

1. Recall three objectives of a formalized risk analysis procedure.
2. Describe the relation of risk analysis to the corporate security program.
3. List the major functions of risk management.
4. Review the three major components of the risk analysis process.

4

Risk Analysis Components

Introduction

Risk analysis is the process by which potentially harmful events are identified, their likelihood estimated, and the impact of their occurrences evaluated. In this topic, you will learn the concepts and the components of the risk analysis process. The risk analysis components are: an asset analysis, threat analysis, vulnerability analysis, and a risk assessment. For each of these risk analysis sub-functions, there are definitions, guidelines, and procedures which are fundamental to becoming a knowledgeable member of a risk analysis project team. After these concepts have been covered in this topic, the actual planning and execution of a risk analysis will be addressed.

TOPIC 1 WHAT IS RISK?

A good definition would be:

"The potential for loss of assets resulting from uncertain harmful events."

Risk occurs when things of value, *assets*, are exposed to harm from some *threat* because of a system, procedural, or environmental *vulnerability*. Risk is some function of the probability of a harmful event and the impact of the harmful event. In its simple and most desirable form, the function is that of multiplication. This leads to the traditional statement of:

$$\text{EXPECTED LOSS} = \text{LOSS PROBABILITY} \times \text{LOSS VALUE}$$

As we continue, you will see that risk situations are not always simple, and the multiplication function may not be adequate. The risk analysis team may *derive* the proper function.

I. Function of Risk Analysis

Risk analysis looks for the coincidence of *assets*, *threats*, and *vulnerabilities* which could result in a harmful event and subsequent corporate loss.

Consider the following examples:

1. Threat—inept employee
   Vulnerability—inadequate edits
   Harmful event—errors in data
2. Threat—fire
   Vulnerability—untested smoke alarm
   Harmful event—machine room fire
3. Threat—system intruders
   Vulnerability—poor access control
   Harmful event—system penetration

Asset analysis identifies the valuable entities of the organization. These assets may include blank purchase-order forms as well as the computer. *Threat analysis* defines the hazards to be considered. *Vulnerability analysis* identifies characteristics of the environment by which threats act upon assets.

II. Function of Risk Assessment

Risk assessment puts it all together. Harmful events are projected, based upon analysis of assets, threats, and vulnerabilities. The measure of potential loss is stated.

What is a *threat*?

"A threat is an aspect of the environment that, when given an opportunity, could cause a harmful event by acting upon an asset."

We are concerned with two kinds of threats: intentional and unintentional, or probabilistic.

1. Algorithmic, or *intentional*, threats are hostile, motivated acts. They may have destructive or fraudulent goals.

Theft is a motivation for algorithmic threat, with the targets defined as:

1. Data
2. Services
3. Equipment

Malice is also a motivation for algorithmic threats. Examples of malicious harmful events are:

1. Sabotage
2. Revenge
3. Vandalism

A government study of identified fraudulent computer crime found that direct payments and actions that attack inventory are the most common. In many organizations, use of facilities for personal benefit has become a way of life or a "fringe benefit." Such usage, even for games, should be considered a threat. In many instances, such threats may develop into more harmful events.

A final form of intentional threat is that of strategic attack. This is a concern because guerrilla or terrorist attacks have occurred at European data centers. A national military emergency could pose threats both from destruction and from residual effects such as radiological contamination.

2. Probabilistic, or *unintentional*, threats are associated with accidents, human error, or environmental hazards and failures. Human error is a type of unintentional threat, as we all make mistakes with some degree of measurable probability.

Some examples of probabilistic threats are:

1. Keystroke errors
2. Procedural errors
3. Programming errors

Equipment failure of the computer or its support system is a probabilistic threat. As a rule, the likelihood of such threats is relatively easy to obtain from equipment records.

A final category of probabilistic threat is that of physical hazards. Threats of this type are generally of considerable interest to personnel whose job is recovery and continuity of operations. Because of this, the

risk analysis team should coordinate efforts against such threats early in the project.

III. The Role of the Risk Analysis Team

The risk analysis team must evaluate the level of threats during their analysis. For unintentional (probabilistic) threats, the probability of occurrence is a good measure of threat level. However, other factors predominate when intentional threats are measured:

1. The actual or perceived value to the thief, vandal, or hostile person.
2. The opportunity for attack.
3. The level of sophistication of the intruder.

All of these factors contribute to the threat level present from intentional threats.

Data to support the analysis may be difficult to obtain. However, data on natural hazards and accidents can be compiled from almanacs, weather records, insurance company reports, and books of similar nature. In estimating the impact of hard-to-handle threats, an approach might be to collect successive estimates of events based on the opinions of experts in the field.

More specifically, let us consider what various examples of penetration to data security could be:

1. Physical penetration techniques include breaking and entering, destruction of property, and theft.
2. Personnel techniques may include bribery or blackmail to cause employees to aid penetration.
3. Hardware techniques might involve wire-tapping, jamming devices, or remote terminals.
4. Software methods of penetration are many; some examples are logic bombs and Trojan horses.
5. Use of a terminal left "operational" during lunch hour is an example of procedural penetration.

IV. Topic Review

1. Review the definition of systems security threat.
2. Recall the two major threat categories.
3. Explain how knowledge of threat types can categorize any type of systems security threat.
4. Review the definition of system security vulnerabilities.
5. List the factors which contribute to vulnerability level.

TOPIC 2 PLANNING A RISK ANALYSIS

Introduction

In the previous topics, the role of risk analysis in a security program, risk analysis concepts, and the management and theoretical aspects of risk analysis were presented. This topic will explain the procedural skills for planning a risk analysis. A risk analysis, particularly one of the data center or of a major system, is a project; it should be managed like any other project. In this topic, you will learn methods for defining the problem, selecting an approach, and properly planning the risk analysis. Guidelines for preparing a risk analysis task plan and getting the project team organized will be presented. As in any complex project, good plans prevent poor performance.

I. Defining the Problem

The problem definition should establish the *who*, *what*, *where*, *when*, and *how* of the project.

Formalizing major work activities at this point should remain at a fairly high level of the top-down approach. During problem definition, the skeleton is still being built. Detail will be added when writing of the task plan is accomplished.

The essential *what*, *who*, and *where* of the problem requires that the following assets or corporate elements must be identified:

1. Facilities

These are the physical entities of the environment, such as security alarms, utility back-ups, and real property.

2. Hardware

These assets include terminals, computers, and associated equipment.

3. Software

Software assets generally exceed hardware in value and consist of both system and application programs.

4. Media and Supplies

Stocks of blank forms, tapes, and paper are examples of media assets.

5. Data

These assets may be on storage media, input forms, or output listings.

6. Employees

Obviously, employees are assets.

7. Communications

Corporate networks and internal data processing links are examples of communications.

II. Personnel

Individuals performing disaster recovery and continuity of operations functions must become involved with the risk analysis project. In addition, the data security administrator and the individuals responsible for physical security should have full-time representatives on the risk analysis team. In the final analysis, a team should be selected which has the skill and experience to fit the approach. All members should be screened prior to selection, and interviews can be conducted, if necessary.

All individual members of the risk analysis team must be clearly aware of their job function and how it relates to the proposed achievement of the overall project.

III. *Selecting the Approach*

When deciding on an approach, the risk analysis team leader must define the scope of the analysis and tailor the approach with the knowledge that certain factors interact and require continuous attention.

The project manager's judicious management of these aspects of the project will, to a large extent, determine the degree of success achieved. Each project aspect, such as people and resources, must be closely considered when deciding on an approach. Otherwise, the project plan may become a plan for failure.

A. Defining the Scope

The following specific guidelines will help you define the scope of your project:

1. Classic guidance is to "think like a thief." How would you select targets and how would you attack them?
2. Investigate the flow of assets into and out of the system. Look for places where inventories or data could leak or be siphoned.
3. Sometimes it is helpful to forget the automated systems and just review the assets that the functional user manages with the system.
4. Conduct an inventory of the systems and data that may be subject to loss.
5. Estimate the size of the risk analysis project in terms of number of data centers, locations, systems, and databases.
6. Based on the size of the project, determine the size of the work effort to be performed involving the following considerations:
   People
   Cost
   Travel
   Technical Support

To summarize:

– "Think like a thief"
– Look at the flow of assets

- Inventory functional assets
- Estimate size of work effort
- Determine corporate and environmental constraints

B. Alternative Technical Approaches

Other recommended approaches to be considered are:

1. **Geographical**—This approach breaks the risk analysis environment into geographical locations such as machine room, warehouse terminals, and archive library. The risk analysis is performed by visiting and analyzing each geographical location.
2. **Organizational**—This approach analyzes major data flows from the perspective of organizational entities. Organizational charts and functions are used to identify the areas to be considered. Such an approach might identify the Data Entry Branch, Software Division, and Office of Operations and Support as the primary sites for the risk analysis.
3. **Input, Process, Storage, Output**—This technical approach breaks each major data flow into its input, process, storage, and output components, and structures the risk analysis accordingly. In most instances, this technical approach provides a straightforward, comprehensive framework for the risk analysis. It is a highly recommended procedure.

IV. *Formalizing the Approach*

A. The Risk Analysis Charter

After a clear problem definition has been produced, it should be formalized in a risk analysis charter. This charter establishes the risk analysis team's authority and provides formal recognition for its mission. After being reviewed by higher management, it should be signed by an individual sufficiently high up in the corporate hierarchy to leave no doubt that the team and its project have management's blessing.

The risk analysis charter should:

1. State who, what, where, when, and how
2. Establish authority
3. Specify lines of reporting
4. Establish claim to resources

5. Prescribe constraints
6. Identify deliverables and milestones

B. The Task Plan

Writing a task plan is the best way to formalize the selected approach. It specifically identifies *what* must be done, by *whom*, and *when*. In developing this plan, major work events identified earlier during problem definition are expanded in detail. Sub-activities within these events are focused on.

It will be noted that some of the identified tasks may be dependent upon the completion of others. When scheduling tasks, the normally available work forces will be the controlling factor, with consideration given to specialized talents.

V. Delivering the Product

Planning a risk analysis project also involves planning a deliverable product. Some examples of these are:

1. **Final Report**—may include list of harmful events, their expected loss potential or other likelihood, and loss estimates.
2. **Functional Reports**—often desirable to highlight major functional areas, such as accounts receivable, in a Functional Area Report.
3. **Periodic Reports**—monthly or weekly progress reports.
4. **Quick-fix Reports**—if major risks are uncovered, a rapid "spot report" or "quick-fix" report may be called for.

VI. Topic Review

1. Review the corporate elements which need to be identified when defining the problem.
2. List some considerations to help determine the scope of a project.
3. Recall the important elements which should be contained in the risk analysis charter.

5

Conducting a Risk Analysis

Introduction

There are as many formal risk analysis formats as there are authors in the field. One of the reasons for this is that the industry has not agreed upon an acceptable method of performing and documenting risk analysis. In this text, the example of risk analysis documentation used is based on a synthesis of the recognized techniques. It emphasizes the need for any risk analysis to provide enough information to permit the derivation of a set of system functional requirements that will later drive a design project.

TOPIC 1 WHAT IS NECESSARY

I. Documentation

We will review what the example of documentation means in terms of what requirements or countermeasures are implied.

A. Organization

    1. Sections by functional cell
    2. Summary risk chart
    3. Risk summary Checksheet
    4. Detailed risk documentation

B. The Risk Summary Chart

1. Threat category
2. Vulnerability
3. Harmful event
4. Probability of occurrence of event
5. Impact summary
6. Risk
7. Indexes

C. Interpreting Results

1. Indexing the risk entries
2. Risk ranking

II. Examples

Examples of the comprehensive forms used in gathering and documenting risk analysis data are shown in the following pages.

The Asset Analysis form is completed for each major data flow identified. (See Figure 5.1.)

Assets, as they are identified, should be entered in the appropriate column along with their values.

Assets may appear in more than one column if necessary to describe the use of assets by the data flow.

Remember that for a major data flow, an asset is anything of value. In the input column, a keystroke device is an asset and so is the purchase order that is keystroked.

In completing the columns, remember to use the functional as well as the data processing perspective.

Perform a survey of each function "CELL."

1. Principles:

Guided by checksheet/checklists/experience.
Uses multidisciplinary expertise.
Requires special skills.

2. Procedures:

Assess threats vs. assets.
Use quantitative data where possible.
Use qualitative estimates if needed.

	Input	Process	Storage	Output
Major Data Flow 1				
Major Data Flow 2				
Major Data Flow 3				

Figure 5.1. Risk analysis procedure—"XYZ" D.P. organization.

3. Documentation:

Use consistent format.
Report quantitative, qualitative, and backup information.

Perform Overall Risk Assessment.

1. Risk Survey Checksheet (Figure 5.2) is a job aid for conducting the threat and vulnerability analyses and for constructing harmful events.
2. One checksheet is completed for each cell of the data flow matrix.
3. Enter in each cell of the checksheet an index number that identifies potentially harmful events.

RISK SURVEY CHECKSHEET

(Indexes to Detail Descriptions)

Major Subsystem _____

Functional Cell _____

Vulnerability Areas

Threat Category		Data	Software	Hardware	Physical Plant	Media & Supplies	People	Commo	Other
Probabilistic	Natural Hazards								
	Equipment Failure								
	Human Error								
Algorithmic	Theft								
	Fraud								
	Malice								
	Strategic Attack								

Figure 5.2. Risk Survey Checksheet.

RISK ESTIMATE DETAIL SHEET

INDEX # _____

HARMFUL EVENT EXPLANATION:

EVENT PROBABILITY ESTIMATE:

IMPACT ESTIMATE:

Figure 5.3. The Risk Detail Sheet is used to record harmful events as they are developed and to estimate likelihood and impact. The index on the detail sheet is the same as the index on the checksheet in Figure 5.2.

RISK SURVEY CHECKSHEET

(Indexes to Detail Descriptions)

Major Subsystem   PAYMIS

Functional Cell   PAYROLL

Vulnerability Areas

Threat Category		Data	Software	Hardware	Physical Plant	Media & Supplies	People	Commo	Other
Probabilistic	Natural Hazards			3					
	Equipment Failure				10, 13			4	
	Human Error	1, 23							
Algorithmic	Theft				5		8,9		
	Fraud	2							
	Malice				6,7				
	Strategic Attack								

Figure 5.4. An example of a partially completed Risk Survey Checksheet. The indices of 12 harmful events are shown. Harmful event #2 describes a potential fraudulent act on data and will be shown on the next page. Note the checksheet covers the "Payroll" function area.

RISK ESTIMATE DETAIL SHEET

INDEX #2

HARMFUL EVENT EXPLANATION:

Overtime hours and pay raise transactions may be fraudulently entered by any employee with logon privileges and payroll office password.

EVENT PROBABILITY ESTIMATE: MEDIUM

Over 70 employees have TSO privileges on their user's code access list. Of these many have partial knowledge of procedures used by the payroll systems.

IMPACT ESTIMATE: LOW

Any drastic changes in the payroll system totals would trigger audit functions and result in warning messages to payroll reviewers before paychecks are distributed.

Figure 5.5. This example of a Risk Estimate Detail Sheet shows how Harmful Event #2 from the previous page might be recorded. Note the example is using fuzzy descriptors for estimates. What are some other ways these estimates could have been described?

RISK

$RISK = F(P_{HE}, I_{HE})$

Unintentional

$P_{HE} = P(Occurrence)$

$I_{HE} = F(Type\ of\ effect,\ asset\ importance,\ current\ security)$

$RISK = P_{HE} \times I_{HE}$

Intentional

$P_{HE} = F(T,V)$

$T = F(Value\ to\ penetrator,\ opportunity\ sophistication)$

$V = F(Current\ security,\ system\ complexity)$

$I = F(Type\ of\ effect,\ asset\ importance,\ current\ security)$

$RISK = F(Threat = HI,\ Vulnerability = MED,\ Impact = HI)$

$RISK = HI$

Figure 5.6. These formulae for risk will be described in more detail in Chapter 6. Risk is a function of the probability of event occurrence and its impact. Record estimates of risk factors on the detail sheets. Be as quantitative as possible, but avoid being precisely inaccurate.

- **Annual Loss Exposure (ALE)**

- **Risk Impact Measurement (RIM)**

- **Tabular Categorization**

- **Fuzzymetrics**

Figure 5.7. Risk qualification methods. A more detailed explanation follows:

1. Annualized Loss Expectancy uses the multiplication function to combine P_{HE} and I_{HE}. It is the simplest and best understood method.

   1.1 ALE results are the easiest to interpret.

   1.2 Numeric estimates of factors are required.

2. Risk Impact Measurement produces a single index based on analysis of threats and vulnerability.

   2.1 Index is relative rather than absolute. It may be difficult to interpret in the real world.

   2.2 Input data to RIM is copious and may be more difficult to estimate than P_{HE} and I_{HE}.

3. Tabular Categorization builds a table with rows of P_{HE} and I_{HE}. The cells are a user defined risk function.

   3.1 Uses the FIPS 65 approach.

   3.2 User specifies the functional relation to be placed in the table.

4. Fuzzymetrics recognizes the difficulty of precise estimates.

   4.1 Uses fuzzy quantifiers like "HIGH," "MEDIUM," or "LOW" for P_{HE} and I_{HE}.

   4.2 Fuzzies can be combined in a tabular categorization.

RISK SUMMARY CHART

Major Subsystem INVENTORY

Functional Cell UBOYT

Threat Category	System Vulnerability Description	Harmful Event Description	Index #	Event Prob # Occ/Yr (Rating)	Impact $ Cost/Occ (Rating)	Risk Level (ALE) (Rating)

Figure 5.8. The framework of your report should be the Risk Survey Checksheet and the Risk Estimate Detail Sheet. The Risk Summary Chart provides an excellent format to pull the facts together.

REPORT PREPARATION

- **Risk Survey Checklist**

- **Risk Estimate Detail Sheet**

- **Risk Summary Chart**

Figure 5.9. Components of a risk analysis report.

The Risk Summary Chart provides for summarization of the primary outputs of the Risk Analysis.

Checksheets and Detail Sheets provide inputs for completing the Summary Chart.

The Chart may be made as quantitative as desired.

The index number points interested persons back into the Detail Sheets where they can find the level of details they desire.

III. *Summary*

Remember the criteria for a good risk analysis:

1. Comprehensive
2. Understandable
3. Technically Sound

The procedures you have learned in this course will produce the risk analysis which meets these criteria. Your report must demonstrate you have attained these standards.

The report may be used by multi-level users and must be understandable to each. This may require several different approaches to reporting results, such as management summaries, descriptive tables, and numeric tables.

IV. *Topic Review*

1. Recall the requirements for Risk Analysis documentation.
2. For report preparation, list the essential forms to be completed.

TOPIC 2   RISK ANALYSIS BY DETAIL

I. *Threat Analysis*

Understanding what elements of the environment pose a threat to the data processing mission is a prerequisite to analysis of risk. Threat analysis is the "function that identifies things that can cause harm and attaches some measure of the threat importance to the organization's mission."

A. Threat Definition

"A THREAT is an aspect of the environment that, when given an opportunity, can cause a harmful event by acting upon an asset."

"A HARMFUL EVENT is a partial or complete loss of a corporate asset."

B. Categories of Threats

Threats can be viewed as falling into two different categories depending on the motivation behind them. One class is made up of threats that are intentional and are performed by people seeking to harm the organization by stealing or disrupting assets. These are called ALGORITHMIC THREATS. Falling into this category would be fraud, theft, malice, and strategic attack.

The second class is made up of threats that seemingly happen by accident. These are called PROBABILISTIC THREATS. Human error may precipitate probabilistic threats involving procedures, programs, systems software, and also equipment failure encompassing computer and/or support equipment. Also included in this category are physical hazards with serious consequence, e.g., storms, power loss, earthquakes, flooding, water damage, fire, and riots.

These two categories frequently require different types of responses from an organization in order to provide maximum defense.

C. Threat Experience

Robert Courtney, of Robert Courtney Associates, has identified a list of what he considers to be the six most severe threats. Those threats in rank order are:

1. Errors and omissions
2. Dishonest employees
3. Fire
4. Disgruntled employees
5. Water
6. Strangers

D. Calculating Levels of Threat

1. T Level (probabilistic) = f(Pocc)
2. T Level (algorithmic) = f(value to penetrator, opportunity of penetrator, sophistication of penetrator)

II. *Vulnerability Analysis*

Definition:

"Vulnerability is a characteristic of a system that could allow a threat to act upon an asset, causing a harmful event."

A. Avenue of Approach

1. Exposure
2. Hole in system defenses
3. Opportunity

B. Factors in Vulnerability Level

1. Complexity of the target asset
2. Current security defenses surrounding asset

C. Identifying Vulnerabilities

1. Vulnerabilities are characteristics of the system environment. They exist because of corporate acts of omission or commission.
2. Threats capitalize upon system vulnerabilities to breach safeguards and to cause a loss.
3. Complex systems are likely to have a higher level of vulnerability than simple systems. Complex systems offer more holes or exposures to harm. Often no one really understands the complex system and can certify it as secure.
4. The level of vulnerability is also dependent upon current security practices. The actions and procedures being taken to prevent harmful events are a determining factor in the vulnerability level.
5. Assets have vulnerabilities.

D. Penetration Techniques

1. Tiger teams
2. Asynchronous
3. Browsing
4. Between the lines
5. Trojan horse
6. Unexpected operations
7. Unexpected parameters
8. Wire tapping

The effects of vulnerabilities may be seen in several impacts.

1. Inability to process may lead to partial or complete loss of service.
2. Data vulnerabilities can lead to privacy violation, corporate embarrassment, or financial losses.
3. Because of a vulnerability, real property may be stolen or destroyed.
4. A vulnerability in the data center could lead to unauthorized disclosure by theft of tapes or listings, or by penetration of the system.

During the vulnerability analysis, the team should look for these overt signs of vulnerabilities.

Historically, flaws and vulnerabilities occur most commonly in these areas. See Figure 5.10.

Consider the implication of the following harmful event. The system software vulnerability is uncontrolled access by system pro-

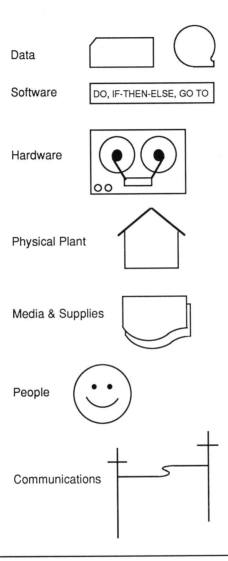

Data

Software

Hardware

Physical Plant

Media & Supplies

People

Communications

Figure 5.10. Vulnerability areas.

grammers to the production library. The threat is a disgruntled systems programmer. Suppose several lines of code are embedded in the system which cause the user code and password to be written to the programmer's file each time the payroll system is executed. The programmer could use multiple combinations of codes and passwords to enter overtime and raise pay data in selected payroll.

During the vulnerability analysis, the project team may see many overt symptoms of existing vulnerabilities.

These symptoms can be used to help identify the basic vulnerability. The historical profile of vulnerabilities in computer systems is:

- System Software
- Operational Procedures
- Telecommunications
- System/User Interfaces
- Industrial Security

III. Impact Analysis

A. Definition

"The measure of the amount of loss from a harmful event is the impact." The levels of threat and vulnerability determine whether or not a harmful event will occur, but say nothing of the effect that the event will have on the organization's mission. Predicting the impact of a hypothetical threat occurrence requires analysis of several factors.

B. Factors of Impact Level

1. Type of effect

    a. Loss of asset: data, programs, services, physical property.
    b. Disruption of asset: data, programs, services, physical property, political damage.
    c. Disclosure of asset.

2. Target asset importance

    a. Kinds of assets
    b. Dollar value

3. Current security

    a. Preventative measures
    b. Containment of effects
    c. Maximizing recovery

To summarize what we have been discussing:

- The levels of threats and vulnerability are the basis for formulating harmful events and estimating their likelihood.

- The risk analysis must also estimate the impact given the occurrence of a harmful event.
- Impact is a measure of the effect of the harmful event.
- Impact is usually expressed in a resource terminology of expected loss. Example: Dollars, employee hours, processing minutes.

IV. *Topic Review*

1. Recall the six most severe threats as defined by Robert Courtney.
2. Identify several possible areas where vulnerabilities might exist.
3. List several penetration techniques.

6

Detail Risk
Assessment

How much impact the occurrence of a harmful event produces is dependent on the nature of the event. Thinking in terms of threat vulnerabilities and impact factors can help in formalizing impact estimates.

A tornado or hurricane can produce large losses of assets and disruption of service. The importance of these corporate assets can be extremely high, such as destruction of the entire data center. Such impact can scarcely be prevented, but good recovery planning can help reduce impact.

Disclosure of an asset, such as the employee salary file, can have an embarrassing impact, but the actual value would probably be minimal.

TOPIC 1 RISK ANALYSIS

I. Definition

"A measure of the potential for loss of assets resulting from uncertain harmful events."

Risk is quantitative by nature: it is an estimate of the amount of impact that can be expected on the average to result from occurrence of uncertain harmful events over a given period of time. To determine risk, we must know what harmful events can happen, the probability of occurrence, and the expected amount of loss if they do occur. Clearly, there are some complex components of this measure, each of which must be identified and quantified. Ideally, we would express risk as an amount of money that would be lost, on an average, over some period of time. A common measure for risk is the Annual Loss Expectancy (ALE). This expresses expected losses as an average yearly dollar figure.

II. The Risk Formula

A. R = f(P(he,), I(he))

The above formula shows risk as a function of the likelihood of a harmful event occurrence and the amount of loss expected from an occurrence. The ALE is normally computed using a multiplication function, where risk is equal to the probability of an occurrence of a harmful event in one year times the dollar value of each event occurrence. Where data is available to support this estimate, it is quite useful. It tells how much an organization can expect to lose; it arranges individual risk in a priority rank by dollar value; and indicates the amount of money that can be justified for construction of defenses to lower the risk. Unfortunately, the probability and cost of a harmful event occurrence cannot always be quantified. When that is the case, the ALE becomes less useful. An alternative to placing numbers in the ALE formula is to assess risk more qualitatively by considering each factor that contributes to the risk level. The formula given above supports that approach by accounting for each risk level component factor in a series of "equations."

B. P(he) = f(T,V)

The probability of occurrence of a harmful event is equal to some function of the level of threat and the level of vulnerability.

C. Tp = P(occ)

The level of threat for a probabilistic threat is equal to the probability of occurrence in a specified time period.

Ta = f(Value to Penetrator, Opportunity to Penetrator, Sophistication of Penetrator).

The level of threat for an algorithmic threat is a function of three different components. The first is a value of a target asset to a potential penetrator. Second is the level of opportunity for a penetrator to commit a harmful event. Finally, sophistication of the penetrator must be considered.

D. V = f(Target Exposure, Current Preventive Security)

The level of vulnerability has two components. First, the amount of exposure of assets in the target system must be considered. Additionally, the currently preventive security features surrounding the system assets must be accounted for.

E. I = f(Type of Effect, Target Importance, Security to "Contain" Effect, Security to Recover)

Ideally, impact would be expressed as dollar value. Each of the impact factors shown above must be considered in assessing a qualitative or quantitative impact value.

III. Topic Review

1. Explain the basic concepts of Risk Assessment.
2. Recall the generic risk formula.

TOPIC 2   STEPS IN THE RISK ANALYSIS PROCEDURE

Many risk methodologies have been proposed in the literature. (The bibliography references most of these). The objective of each of these is to divide the problem of looking at an organization's security posture into measurable parts. A risk analysis methodology is briefly described here to show how the documentation of risk is derived.

The risk assessment is the melting pot of the risk analysis. Using the asset analysis, the threat analysis, and the vulnerability analysis, it amalgamates these components into harmful events whose probability and impact can be estimated.

The principal outputs are a qualification of expected loss and a ranking by the importance of the harmful event.

The risk assessment is the basis for identifying countermeasures.

As previously discussed, there are many risk analysis methodologies; most produce estimates of expected loss. However, the techniques for risk assessment may differ significantly. Here are two ends of the spectrum.

Procedures used by the government, as presented in FIPS 65 (see Figure 6.1), find expected loss by tabular look-up. The columns give frequency categories. The rows of the table are impact categories. Thus, if a harmful event is expected to occur "once in 100 days" (column 4) and has a $10,000 impact (row 4), the expected loss is at the row-column intersection, i.e., $30,000.

The Stanford Institute's Relative Impact Measure uses the formula shown here:

N_p = number of individuals in proposed perpetrator class p. The user can have a number of classes such as programmers, users, cleaning-persons, and terrorists.

S_p = relative severity rating for the perpetrators in class p. Applications programmers may be considered more dangerous than cleaning persons for a given target (e.g., fraudulent payroll actions).

F_{pt} = probability of vulnerability linking perpetrator class p and target class t.

A_{pt} = relative attractiveness of targets in class t to perpetrators in class p. Thus, portable terminals may be less attractive to terrorists than to a late night worker.

I_t = impact of a successful attack on target t.

Determining risk must always involve a treatment of likelihood and impact.

Risk for harmful events due to unintentional threats should be assessed by procedures different than those used for intentional threats.

Probability of occurrence is usually an adequate measure of likelihood for accidental, natural hazard, and human error harmful events.

For motivated harmful events such as theft, fraud, or malicious destruction, more complex measures for likelihood should be applied.

• FIPS 65

i = \ f =	1 Once in 300 years (100,000 days)	2 Once in 30 Years (10,000 days)	3 Once in 3 years (1,000 days)	4 Once in 100 days	5 Once in 10 days	6 Once per day	7 10 per day	8 100 per day
1 — $10					$300	$3,000		$300k
2 — $100				$300	$3,000	$30k	$300k	$3M
3 — $1000			$300	$3,000	$30k	$300k	$3M	$30M
4 — $10,000		$300	$3,000	$30k	$300k	$3M	$30M	
5 — $100,000	$300	$3,000	$30k	$300k	$3M	$30M	$300M	
6 — $1,000,000	$3,000	$30k	$300k	$3M	$30M	$300M		
7 — $10,000,000	$30k	$300k	$3M	$30M	$300M			
8 — $100,000,000	$300k	$3M	$30M	$300M				

$$RIM = \sum_P N_P \times S_P \sum_T F_{PT} \times A_{PT} \times I_T$$

• SRI

Figure 6.1. Two methods of risk assessment.

RISK

$$\text{RISK} = F(P_{HE}, I_{HE})$$

Unintentional

$$P_{HE} = P(\text{Occurrence})$$

$$I_{HE} = F(\text{Type of effect, asset importance, current security})$$

$$\text{RISK} = P_{HE} \times I_{HE}$$

Intentional

$$P_{HE} = F(T,V)$$

$$T = F(\text{Value to penetrator, opportunity sophistication})$$

$$V = F(\text{Current security, system complexity})$$

$$I = F(\text{Type of effect, asset importance, current security})$$

$$\text{RISK} = F(\text{Threat} = \text{HI, Vulnerability} = \text{MED, Impact} = \text{HI})$$

$$\text{RISK} = \text{HI}$$

Figure 6.2. Types of risk.

Problem 1. During the past two years, the master customer-billing-file has become unreadable 12 times. Apparently operator error in updating the file is responsible, but events surrounding the destruction are such that the exact cause has not been determined. The file can be recreated by processing back up tapes and field-office transaction files. Because of overtime, rescheduling of other work, and processing time, managers of accounts-receivable and the data center estimate the impact at an average cost of $7500 per reprocessing. What is the expected loss for this harmful event?

Problem 2. A risk analysis team has identified five fraudulent harmful events. In analyzing each, the team members have built the table shown below. How can they derive a function to estimate the risk of each event? What is the ranking of the five events using this function?

Harmful Event	P_{HE}	I_H
1	High	Low
2	Medium	High
3	Low	Medium
4	Medium	Medium
5	Low	High

Topic Review

1. List the three main steps in the risk analysis procedure.
2. Be familiar with the contents of the risk analysis report.
3. Describe some other common risk analysis methodologies.

Following are examples of the Risk Summary Chart and the Risk Estimate Detail Sheet.

RISK SUMMARY CHART

Major Subsystem   PERSONNEL

Functional Cell   PROCESS

Threat Category	System Vulnerability Description	Harmful Event Description	Index #	Event Prob # Occ/Yr (Rating)	Impact $ Cost/Occ (Rating)	Risk Level (ALE) (Rating)
Fraud	Applications programs have unlimited data access within a file	Penetrator could circumvent the system access licensing mechanism by writing unauthorized programs	22	3	1	2
	Passwords are maintained on a file with file level security and no protective transforms	Program with password keys can print out the password tables	23	3	5	4
		Password tables could appear on a system memory dump and be compromised	24	2	5	4
	Console operator can display any memory location contents on system console and system generation link edit output is not controlled	Password tables and protected data are accessed by system operator	25	2	5	4
	Production application program library is accessible to all programmers and anyone with file names and access keys	Changes to production program to install unauthorized "Trojan Horse" code	26	3	4	4
		Changes to disable edits or production features	27	3	4	4

Figure 6.3. Risk Summary Chart example.

RISK ESTIMATE DETAIL SHEET

INDEX #22

HARMFUL EVENT EXPLANATION:

Access to data files is generally restricted at the file level by operating system access keys. Access to data within a single file is controlled by applications program: an application program can access all of any file for which the keys are known. An application program could be written to allow user access to entire files even when the user is not cleared for some data elements.

EVENT PROBABILITY ESTIMATE: Rating = 3 (MEDIUM)

IMPACT ESTIMATE: Rating = 1 (LOW)

Impact would be low since few files are internally partitioned into elements with different access limits.

RISK ESTIMATE DETAIL SHEET

INDEX #23

HARMFUL EVENT EXPLANATION:

Password tables used to limit user access to terminals are maintained on a system file with locks but no other protection. A penetrator who discovered the file keys could print all passwords in the table.

EVENT PROBABILITY ESTIMATE: Rating = 3 (MEDIUM)

Limited numbers of people have access to the password file keys but risk compromise is substantial.

IMPACT ESTIMATE: Rating = 5 (CRITICAL)

Successful penetration of password tables could expose many of the most important systems, including payroll processing.

RISK ESTIMATE DETAIL SHEET

INDEX #24

HARMFUL EVENT EXPLANATION:

Password tables occasionally appear on system memory dumps. The personnel/payroll system password tables are similarly exposed. Hardcopy memory dumps are not well controlled while being printed, stored, and used. Password table could be compromised.

EVENT PROBABILITY ESTIMATE: Rating = 2 (LOW)

IMPACT ESTIMATE: Rating = 5 (CRITICAL)

(See Index #23)

RISK ESTIMATE DETAIL SHEET

INDEX #25

HARMFUL EVENT EXPLANATION:

Console operator can display any memory location contents. Access to printed cross-reference tables showing memory location to tables including passwords is not controlled. A knowledgeable operator could access all user passwords and be able to manipulate personnel or payroll data.

EVENT PROBABILITY ESTIMATE: Rating = 2 (LOW)

IMPACT ESTIMATE: Rating = 5 (CRITICAL)

Compromise of passwords is the most serious effect. Operators would have limited ability to affect stored data.

RISK ESTIMATE DETAIL SHEET

INDEX #26

HARMFUL EVENT EXPLANATION:

Changes could be placed in the source code of production programs, or unauthorized programs could be placed on the executable library to perform fraudulent actions upon request by a penetrator.

EVENT PROBABILITY ESTIMATE: Rating = 3 (MEDIUM)

There is so little preventive security that a relatively unsophisticated fraud could be successful.

IMPACT ESTIMATE: Rating = 4 (HIGH)

Effect could be costly (fraudulent payroll actions) and could be damaging to the morale of the employees (disclosure of personal data).

RISK ESTIMATE DETAIL SHEET

INDEX #27

HARMFUL EVENT EXPLANATION:

Changes could be made to disable edits on transactions or to disable password protection.

EVENT PROBABILITY ESTIMATE: Rating = 3 (MEDIUM)

(See Index #26)

IMPACT ESTIMATE: Rating = 4 (HIGH)

(See Index #26)

7

Management's Role

Introduction

You will recall that the overall risk management model discussed called for management review and decision after the risk analysis. It is reasonable to assume that the work of the risk analysis team may continue into this phase of the overall security program. This topic considers the presentation of the risk analysis results to management and the translation of the risk analysis into functional requirements statements.

TOPIC 1 MANAGEMENT REVIEW

I. Presentation

Presentation to management of the risk analysis team's conclusions must inspire confidence and demonstrate the professionalism of the team. No matter how good the risk analysis *really* is, if management's perception of it is poor, then overall utility is likely to suffer.

II. Objectives

The management decision phase has the following objectives:

1. Evaluate identified risks as to degree of acceptability. As a certain degree of risk will always be present in a large, complex

system, the success of risk management depends on the evaluation of identified risks.

2. Select cost-effective countermeasures. Normally several approaches to counter risks will be apparent. Management must select those which are cost-effective.

3. Set priorities for implementing countermeasures. As risk analysis usually identifies many more hazards than can be corrected immediately, managers must establish priorities for countermeasures.

4. Define constraints on countermeasures. Limits to hazard counteraction must be set by management.

III. Role of Risk Analysis Team

During the management decision phase, the risk analysis team continues to function in an important way. As a member of the risk analysis team, you may be called upon to lead your managers through the decision process. The risk review begins with report reading, but should continue with a joint work group review by managers of the functional user, data processing, and security. These managers may look to you to structure the problem and to formulate options.

While management is involved in this decision phase, the risk analysis team may be consulted to perform other activities to assist in decision-making. More specifically, because of the team's expertise and knowledge gained during the analysis, managers may want the team's assistance in implementing countermeasures.

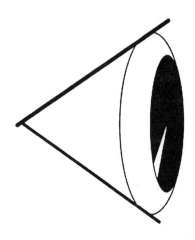

IV. *Follow-up Activities*

As part of the active management review and decision phase, certain follow-up activities may be required of the risk analysis team. Some examples of these requests are:

- Verbal presentations
- More definitive analysis
- Implementation guidance
- Formulation of alternative countermeasures
- Cost analysis of countermeasures

V. *Topic Review*

1. Recall the objectives of the management decision phase.
2. Review the functions of the risk analysis team during the management decision phase.

TOPIC 2 FUNCTIONAL REQUIREMENTS FOR DESIGN

Introduction

When the risk analysis is completed, a set of countermeasures must be designed to respond to the risks that are documented as being most important. The technology of countermeasure construction has some unfamiliar and occasionally complex aspects. The problem need

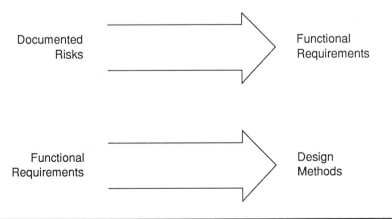

Figure 7.1. Flow from risks to design.

not be so formidable, however, if the knowledge we have of systems development methodology can be applied.

The discipline of systems development can be directly applied to the countermeasures development process. We can define functional requirements and then design and implement "features" that satisfy the requirements. There are some new and possibly unfamiliar tools to be used in the countermeasures development process; these are the special technologies used to implement countermeasures.

I. Security Requirements Specification

The risks documented in the risk analysis report can be used to generate functional requirements for countermeasure design. These requirements will be treated exactly like more familiar functional requirements in a system development context. The risk analysis report is a good starting point for finding the risk elements that must be addressed. When specifying the design requirements, it is desirable to include some detail on the level and kind of security needed. For this, the risk detailed description must be consulted.

II. Generating the Requirements

A. Types of Security Countermeasures

To generate requirements, one must review each documented risk, and specify requirements for reducing that risk. Each requirement must specify the risk being addressed, the kind of security to be provided, and the level of security needed.

1. **"Preventive" Security:** prevent harmful events from occurring at all. A major part of fire precaution should be preventive, and this is just as important with all other security breaches. Would-be embezzlers should be discouraged from ever beginning.

2. **"Containment" Security:** minimize the damage if it does happen. An intruder who succeeds in bypassing the physical or programmed controls that were intended to keep him out should still be very restricted in what he can accomplish. A fire, once started, should be prevented from spreading. A disk that has been dropped and bent should be prevented from damaging a read head, which in turn could damage other disks. If the security procedures are compromised, it must be

possible to limit the harm that could result. Some security designers have made the grave error of supposing that their preventive measures will always work.

3. **"Recovery" Security:** design a method of recovering from the damage. It must be possible to reconstruct vital records or whole files if they become accidentally or willfully damaged or lost. It must be possible to recover from a disastrous fire sufficiently quickly to keep the business running. If an unauthorized person obtains a security code or a file of security codes, it must be possible to change these quickly so that they are of no use to him/her. It is important to attack the security problem in depth, and recovery procedures are vital to the overall plan. The designers must not be allowed to become so infatuated with their preventive mechanisms that they neglect recovery techniques.

B. Format of the Functional Requirements

1. Requirement statement
2. Security type indicated
3. Guidelines for level of security (design constraints)

III. *Other Considerations*

Consideration should be given to the service provided by the system when utilizing countermeasures; the quality must not be degraded. In larger operational systems, a realistic constraint may mean that the countermeasure requires no change to the existing data structure. A stronger constraint than no degradation is that of transparency; the system user should not be aware that a countermeasure is in effect.

Constraints of cost and time are self-explanatory, but do not forget that a countermeasure can have both implementation and operation cost and time elements.

The Functional Security Requirements Worksheet (Figure 7.2) is the recommended form for writing functional requirements statements.

1. The index number and harmful event information comes from the Risk Estimate Detail Sheet.
2. The requirements statement should contain an action verb indicating the level of security, such as "PREVENT . . ." or "CONTAIN . . ."

FUNCTIONAL SECURITY REQUIREMENTS WORKSHEET

INDEX # _____

HARMFUL EVENT DESCRIPTION:

SYSTEM FUNCTIONAL AREAS AFFECTED:

PROBABILITY AND IMPACT:

CONSTRAINTS:

REQUIREMENTS STATEMENT:

Figure 7.2. Functional Security Requirements Worksheet format.

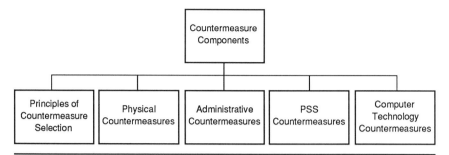

Figure 7.3. Countermeasure components.

IV. Topic Review

1. Describe the three types of security countermeasures.
2. Recall some of the constraints in implementing counter-measures.

8

Selection of Countermeasure Components

Introduction

This chapter presents a discussion of the countermeasures used to provide data security. Once a risk analysis of some form has been conducted, a set of security functional requirements will be developed to correspond with the organizational or system needs. Countermeasures are then selected according to certain criteria to fulfill these requirements.

There are several types of security countermeasures, some of which are appropriate for organization-wide use and some are designed for individual application systems. The basic principle of countermeasures is that the cheapest and simplest countermeasure which will prevent or render an attack on the system too costly to the attacker is the best one to implement. Any system will probably employ several countermeasures to protect against different threats.

Topic 2 of this chapter presents a series of security countermeasures which address risks in the system's environment. The countermeasures have been divided into four categories based on the tools and techniques used to implement them. Topic 2 also discusses Physical, Administrative, and Procedural (PSS) countermeasures.

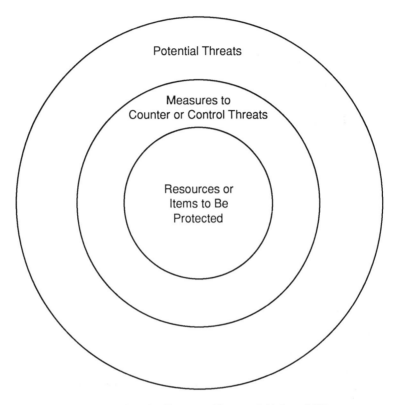

○ Barrier Between Threats & Vulnerabilities
○ Reduce Identified Vulnerabilities
○ Build Efficient Defenses

Figure 8.1. Objectives.

TOPIC 1   PRINCIPLES OF COUNTERMEASURE SELECTION

I. Objectives of Countermeasure Design:

1. Barrier between threats and assets.
2. Reduce identified vulnerabilities.
3. Build efficient defenses.

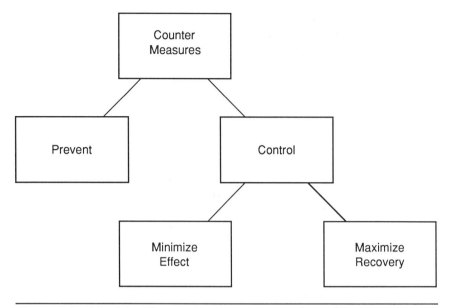

Figure 8.2. Principle: "Countermeasures prevent harmful events or control their effects."

II. Countermeasure Selection Principles

Countermeasures are intended either to prevent or to control harm caused by a threat agent. The threat agent may be intentional (e.g., crime) or unintentional (e.g., human error or natural hazard).

Control countermeasures address the "IMPACT" portion of risk and are intended to:

1. Minimize losses resulting from the attack by discovering and by thwarting it quickly ("CONTAINMENT" security)

   or

2. Maximize recovery from the attack by reducing down-time and recovery expense ("RECOVERY" security). (See Figure 24.)

Note that control countermeasures can actually help deter intentional threats, because the attacker may be caught or his intended impact lessened.

Preventive countermeasures against algorithmic (intentional) threats are based upon making the penetration cost to attacker greater than the expected gain from penetration. Penetration costs consist of:

1. Actual cost of penetration
2. Cost of attack discovery (traceability)
3. Amount of time required for penetration

Potential gain (value of the asset) to the attacker may be different from company's valuation of the asset.

Cost of any countermeasure (one time and recurring) must be less than the expected loss if the countermeasure were not installed.

A recognized functional security requirement may be covered by a number of countermeasures of different types.

Countermeasures with the highest expected payoff should be given selection priority. Payoff is governed by:

1. Reduction of the most costly risks
2. Best ratio of risk reduction versus countermeasure cost
3. Simplicity of the countermeasure (the simpler to use and maintain the better)

Countermeasures may be combined to amplify their individual protective powers.

III. Limitations of Countermeasures

Countermeasures need to be periodically reviewed for effectiveness. Criteria:

1. Continued effectiveness as designed (are the methods and procedures being followed properly).
2. Continued appropriateness (have threats or vulnerabilities changed).
3. Need for other or additional countermeasures.

Every countermeasure has cost associated with it.

1. One time costs:

Purchase of equipment or software
Development of programs and procedures
Installation

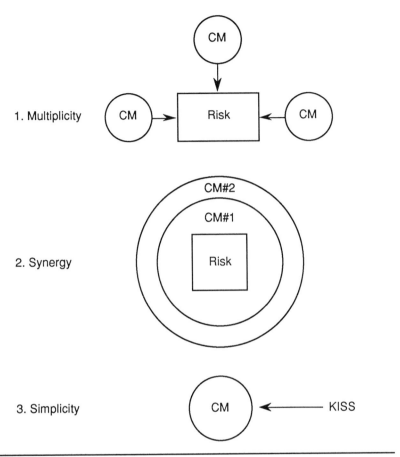

Figure 8.3. Countermeasure selection effectiveness principles.

2. Operating costs:

Degradation of system operation (overhead)
Resources for operation (e.g., power, people)
Maintenance of countermeasure effectiveness (monitor, review,
    modify)

No set of countermeasures can provide complete protection against
all possible threats. Any single countermeasure can be broken by a
determined attacker, given enough time, resources, and ingenuity.

Some basic effectiveness principles to be considered are (See
Figure 8.3.):

1. **Multiplicity:** A functional security requirement may be covered by any of a number of countermeasures of different types. Example: Terminal security via physical lock, operating system lockout, or software access control.
2. **Synergy:** Countermeasures may be combined to amplify their individual protection powers. Example: Use of more than one type of lock described above.
3. **Simplicity:** The simpler the countermeasure, the better, because even countermeasures have "holes" in proportion to their complexity.

IV. Principles of Countermeasure Cost

A. "The cost of any countermeasure must be less than the expected loss if the countermeasure is not installed."

B. "Countermeasures aimed at international threats should make the cost of penetration more than the value obtained from penetration."

V. Countermeasure Effectiveness

There is no sole source in determining the effectiveness of countermeasures. However, it is very important that system designers and developers have *some* idea of the effectiveness of a countermeasure before it is implanted.

After implementation, the effectiveness of a countermeasure does not remain static. Changes in the system vulnerabilities and threats impact the effectiveness of a countermeasure. Therefore, countermeasures must be periodically reviewed and tested, with changes being made if necessary.

VI. Countermeasure Selection Constraints

Some countermeasures may not be usable due to lack of skilled personnel. The training to obtain certain security skills and knowledge is often unavailable or simply "not in the budget." A limited number of operations personnel can make some security functions impossible.

In addition to these problems, your hardware/software combination may not be supported for commercially available software. This is often a problem for the non-IBM user.

Deadlines associated with system development or production schedules often cause security countermeasures to be short-changed. Security too often "gets the axe" when time becomes short.

VII. System Auditability Requirements

Auditability aids in proving the design correctness of the system, as auditability looks forward to the time when the system will be audited. The re-creation of events is fundamental to the examination of the system.

Assistance with auditability requirements often comes from quality assurance.

VIII. Topic Review

1. Recall several general principles that must guide countermeasure selection.
2. Recall several general limitations of countermeasures.

TOPIC 2 SELECT PHYSICAL SECURITY COUNTERMEASURES

Physical security countermeasures form the outermost layer of system protection. For most people, these are the types of countermeasures or actions that come to mind when the word SECURITY is used. They are basically administrative measures intended to guard against any type of physical damage to the system.

The four types of countermeasures are:

1. **Physical**—tangible means of preventing harm, such as locks, guards, building construction.
2. **Administrative**—measures for reducing the hazard or threat from people, such as screening and training.

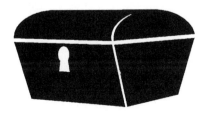

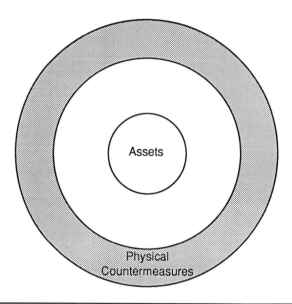

Figure 8.4. Physical countermeasures—The outer layer of security.

3. **Personnel Subsystem**—security procedures to be performed by humans, such as logging and file backup.
4. **Computer Subsystem**—using technical hardware/software methods for security.

I. Guiding Principles

A. Purpose

Physical countermeasures are physical methods of limiting access to equipment, supplies, and media comprising the computer system. They are intended to prevent or give early detection of any type of threat to the physical (not informational) components of the system. These threats may be intentional, such as intents to steal or sabotage, or unintentional, such as natural hazards like fire or power failure.

B. Characteristics

Physical countermeasures are of two general types: the lock, or physical barrier of prevention, and the corrective mechanism which minimizes losses and maximizes ease of recovery. There are numerous possible security functions that can fall under each category. In this course, we will discuss only the most important ones.

C. Limitations

In the modern technological era, physical access to the assets of the computer system is not needed for many serious threats.

The system must be designed for realistic threat levels. It is rarely perfect.

Physical countermeasures tend to be very expensive.

II. *Types of Physical Countermeasures*

A. Physical Access Controls

1. **Definition**
   Physical access controls limit or prevent the access of human threat agents to physical components of the system.
2. **Implementation techniques**
   a. Physical location—reduce exposure of assets by putting them in a less accessible place in the plant.
   b. Security guards and couriers—personal identification is still the best method of access authorization and is a major deterrent.
   c. Locks and alarms—all physical entryways to the important resources should be protected.
   d. Surveillance systems and intrusion detectors—extend the sphere of control of security guards.
   e. Safes—protection of critical media (disks, tapes, documentation) and sensitive data when not in use. Available for burglary protection or fire protection.

B. Hazard Protection

1. **Definition**
   Hazard protection encompasses control methods and equipment used to protect or recover from hazards in the operating environment, either natural or man-made. Man-made hazards

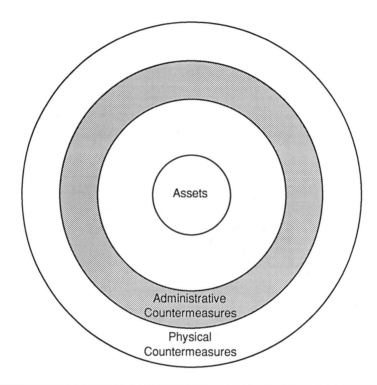

Figure 8.5. Administrative countermeasures—The second layer of security.

may be intentional (e.g., arson) or unintentional (e.g., power failures due to accidents).

2. **Implementation techniques**
   a. Fire prevention and detection measures: combustion sensors, automatic fire extinguishing systems (e.g., Halon), and local and remote alarms.
   b. Power supplies: line monitors to identify power problems, power smoothing devices (e.g., motor-generators or ripple filters), short-period backup power (Uninterruptible Power Supply (UPS)), and long-period backup power (diesel or turbine generators).
   c. Environmental controls (temperature and humidity): sensors, temperature/humidity records, and extra air conditioning units.

    d. Preventing water damage: physical location (away from basements or water sources in upper floors), under-floor water sensors, and equipment covers.

C. Other Physical Countermeasures

Backup equipment and telecommunications
Alternate operational site
Offsite storage of backup critical media (programs and data) and
  supplies
Occupational safety—protecting employees from hazards

III. Topic Review

    1. Give examples of accepted physical security countermeasures.
    2. Review the four types of countermeasures.

TOPIC 3   SELECT ADMINISTRATIVE SECURITY COUNTERMEASURES

Administrative security countermeasures form the second layer of system protection. They are oriented towards shielding the system from nonsecure human elements within the organization.

I. Guiding Principles

A. Purpose

Administrative countermeasures are methods to ensure that personnel who have access to sensitive data are unlikely to compromise it. These methods are basically preventive in nature and are directly aimed at the human aspects without reference to any particular computer system.

B. Characteristics

Administrative countermeasures are of four general types: employee technical training, employee reliability screening, employee security training, and morale enhancement activities. All of these may be carried out in the routine administrative and personnel portions of the company business. They are crucial because company security is based ultimately on employee trustworthiness and reliability. A trustworthy employee who is security conscious and well motivated is more likely to cooperate fully with the company data security program. He/she will form a powerful barrier to security threats.

C. Limitations

Administrative (personnel) security is mainly founded on the principles of human trust and reliability. Humans tend to need periodic reinforcement of these traits, because they may forget sound practices.

Security screening does not rule out the possibility that an employee may later become a threat agent for numerous reasons.

II. Types of Administrative Countermeasures

A. Screening and Bonding of Employees

1. Definition

Screening and bonding encompass a series of actions intended to establish the personal trustworthiness of an employee. This process is also intended to make certain that employees who have access to sensitive information are authorized basic access privileges to information at that level.

2. Implementation techniques

   a. Pre-employment screening—determination by means of investigations with prior employers and other sources that a potential employee can be expected to be trustworthy in the position for which he/she is to be hired.

   b. Bonding of key employees—a form of insurance in which an outside agent insures the company against losses from an employee's untrustworthiness (implies some form of background investigation of the employee by the bonding agent).

   c. Follow-up security checks—for employees working in highly sensitive areas of business, the company may periodically reinvestigate their trustworthiness and do some form of surveillance over their security-related activities.

   d. Defense industrial security clearances—employees working on sensitive defense contracts will be required to undergo investigation prior to being granted security clearances at the appropriate level.

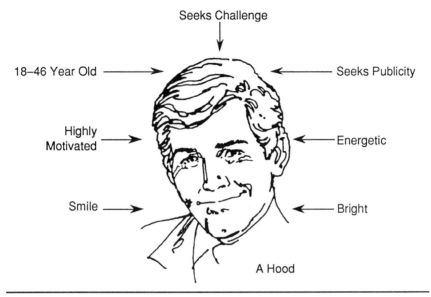

Seeks Challenge

18–46 Year Old

Seeks Publicity

Highly Motivated

Energetic

Smile

Bright

A Hood

Figure 8.6. Profile of a potential computer criminal:
- Reliable
- Honest
- Most desirable employee
- Considers it highly immoral to harm *individuals*

But

- Regards acts of penetration as challenge to skill in beating system
- Not morally concerned with resulting harm inflicted on *organization*

B. Employee Security Education

1. Definition

Employee security education is a formal program of the company intended to create and maintain security awareness among the employees. This includes formal training and morale reinforcement activities.

2. Implementation techniques

a. Security training—training in good security practices for the employee. This training includes general security awareness instruction as well as job-related courses.

b. Personnel conduct codes and other media—general security awareness publications and posters, useful as reminders. EDP professional organizations, such as the ACM and ICCP, promote ethical codes of conduct to which many members adhere. Occasionally, problems may arise between professional and company orientations.

c. Occupational safety and morale maintenance—tools to maintain the employee's morale and identification with the company. A disgruntled or hurt employee has been shown to be a potential security risk.

C. Technical Competency of Employees

The threats to security of data processing operations from incompetent, poorly trained, or careless employees are as severe as deliberate or malicious attempts on the system. Administrative controls should provide for:

Check of the qualifications and skill of all applicants for employment.

Thorough supervision of inexperienced employees.

Special training in areas where employees are found to be deficient.

Performance evaluation of all employees at regular intervals with proper follow-up.

D. Security Administration

1. Definition
Security administration refers to a number of functions which are basic to the company security policy.

2. Implementation techniques
a. Non-disclosure agreements—documents signed by employees and contractors where they accept a legal responsibility not to disclose proprietary or sensitive company information, even if they quit the company.

b. Separation of duties—personnel procedures that reduce the scope of access to sensitive information by any one employee to the minimum needed to perform the job. Includes the idea that more than one person ought to be required to work together in order to do highly sensitive work with the computer system.

    c. Employee terminations—immediately upon termination notice for any reason, employees should be barred from access to sensitive areas and materials. This is a highly important security precaution.

    d. Personal access authorizations—formal procedures to verify that an employee working on sensitive data has the correct clearance level and the need to gain access to specific portions of the data.

I. Topic Review

1. Review accepted administrative security countermeasures.
2. Describe some administrative security countermeasures, including the purpose and limitations of each.

TOPIC 4   SELECT PSS SECURITY COUNTERMEASURES

Procedural security countermeasures are active, functioning parts of a system. In general, there are ways in which the total system is made to operate securely. Procedural countermeasures may belong to both the personnel and computer subsystems (PSS/CSS). A given countermeasure type could be a member of either or both, depending on the nature of the system. This topic will discuss the countermeasures which are commonly implemented in the PSS. A later chapter will be devoted to countermeasures which are ordinarily part of the CSS.

I. Guiding Principles

A. Purpose

PSS countermeasures are people-oriented methods intended to:

1. Reduce the chance for human or system error.
2. Reduce the opportunity for fraud or other intentional threats against any part of the system.
3. Implement active system control and reliability countermeasures in the PSS of application systems.

B. Characteristics

PSS countermeasures are of two general types: those personnel procedures which relate to the computer system as a whole and those

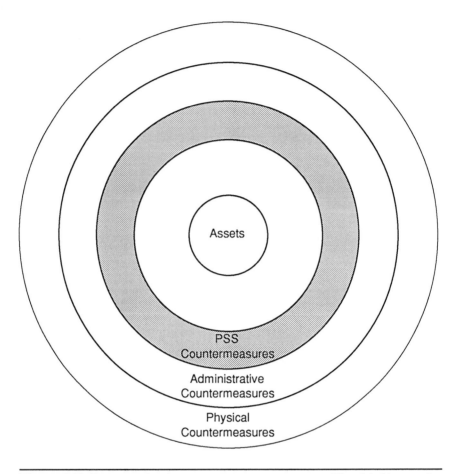

Figure 8.7. Personnel subsystem countermeasures—The third layer of security.

which are a part of individual application systems. The first type is a set of procedures which will be used for every operational system in a data center, because a general need is recognized. The second type will be tailored to the individual security needs of each application system.

C. Limitations

1. Countermeasures may impose complex procedural requirements that can be sources of error and inefficiency.

2. Manual countermeasures can be ineffective against determined attack by relatively unsophisticated individuals.
3. Human factors require continual reinforcement of PSS countermeasures.

II. *Types of PSS Countermeasures*

A. User PSS Controls

1. **Definition**
   User PSS controls are part of an application system and are incorporated into user personnel procedures. They are all manual or relate to man-machine interface components.

2. **Examples of implementation techniques**
   a. Batch controls—manual computation of control field totals on the source documents for comparison with system-generated totals.
   b. Personal accountability—procedures to show which clerk entered each input transaction, so this may be traced if problems occur.
   c. Manual backup procedures—procedures for manual processing of the most critical system functions in the event of a severe automated system failure.
   d. User input/output station operations—control of hard copy input and output materials to restrict access to authorized people, and to perform visual quality checks.
   e. Manual verification of processing—manual simulation of system processing for sample transactions to validate a system's continued reliability.
   f. Straightforward procedural documentation—user procedures for control and system reliability need to be clear and easy to use, if they are to be followed.

B. Data Center PSS Controls

1. **Definition**
   Data Center PSS controls are designed for use by operators and other data center employees to ensure reliability and control of all application systems run.

2. **Examples of implementation techniques**
   a. Data center input/output counter operations—generally the

same as for use I/O, but requires tighter control over pickup/delivery authorization and authentication of user identity. There are two schools of thought regarding how the sensitive input/output activities of a computer center should be organized. Some organizations have chosen the traditional work station concept, where carts of materials are moved from station to station. Other organizations have adopted a traveling team approach where the traveling team is scheduled to the job, does the setup, pulls the tapes, performs the operations, prepares the output, and feeds the distribution system. With the traveling team approach, accountability is precise since the team is in control of the sensitive job at all times.

b. Data library operations—procedures for positive control of magnetic media contents, location, and maintenance (includes erasing sensitive files upon expiration).

c. System crash backup/recovery procedures—procedures for system power-up in secure ways and for restoring operational software correctly.

d. External file label checks—positive verification of mountable media during job setup.

e. Control of operating system utilities—both operators and applications development personnel need to have clearly specified procedures and conditions required for use of powerful system utility programs and routines.

f. Program library procedures—in the absence of an automated program library package, tight controls should be placed over the program library. Test programs should be maintained on libraries separate from the production library, and sign-off authorizations required before new programs are entered into the production library.

g. Continuity of operations procedures—a broad group of countermeasures intended to permit the data center to continue providing essential service even under catastrophic conditions. Includes procedures for data and program copying for offsite storage, backup alternate data center support agreements, and the like.

h. Analysis of job accounting information—computer systems automatically generate logs of system activity (e.g., IBM's SMF), which can give detailed security-related information on terminal usage, file activity, resource utilization, and other performance factors.

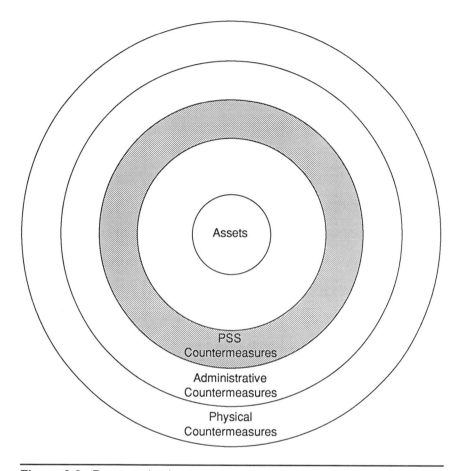

Figure 8.8. Personnel subsystem countermeasures—The third layer of security.

i. Security program procedures—an assemblage of procedures for implementing data system security in the data center. Includes such items as:

Assignment of operators to specific shifts according to job sensitivity

Maintenance of authentication and access authorization password files

Responsibility for review of security logs

Safeguarding telephone numbers of key DPC personnel

Delayed updating of sensitive databases

III. *Topic Review*

1. Review the purpose of PSS countermeasures.
2. Give some examples of user PSS controls and their purpose.
3. Describe in what ways data center implementation of PSS controls can be effective.

9

Select Computer Technology Security Countermeasures

There is a special set of data security countermeasures in which the capabilities of the computer system are used to protect the system itself. This set is called computer technology countermeasures.

The architecture of the system is constructed to include technological barriers, or safeguards, that prevent or detect misuse or malfunction of the system. This chapter will discuss these technological safeguards as they are implemented in each of the components of the system.

Computer technology countermeasures reside in software code, hardware, communications equipment, and the procedures to operate them. These safeguards include automation of countermeasures which can be implemented by manual procedures or physical barriers, as well as functions which are too complex for human execution.

Basic CSS security principles acknowledge that the computer's capabilities can be used to protect itself; barriers and locks within the system can hinder misuse; and automated methods of security are more reliable and consistent.

In this chapter, we will be considering the five types of CSS countermeasures:

1. System software—operating system and associated utility routines
2. Database Management Systems (DBMS)—standard packages for manipulating databases

3. Application software
4. Hardware
5. Communications and terminals

TOPIC 1   SYSTEMS SOFTWARE COUNTERMEASURES

I. *Guiding Principles*

A. Purpose

System software countermeasures are safeguards installed in the operating system and associated utility routines. From a security point of view, the operating system is a critical component of the total computer system. If a knowledgeable attacker can gain control over the operating system, then nearly all of the other system countermeasures can be nullified. The complexity of present large computer operating systems renders them very vulnerable to attack. Consequently, a large amount of contemporary research is devoted to securing operating systems.

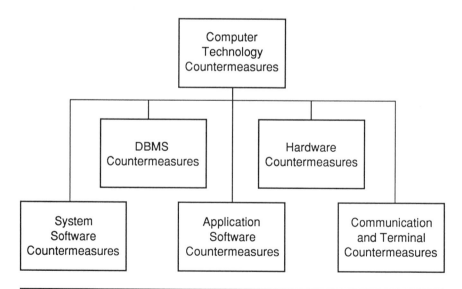

Figure 9.1.

B. Characteristics

System software countermeasures are portions of the operating system code. They are devoted to restricting the access of any system resource (batch job, terminal, etc.) to the minimum legal resources and data needed to do the work, and to preventing any attacker from gaining access to any data or resources.

C. Limitations

Truly secure operating systems in a multiuser environment must be extremely sophisticated.

To date, completely secure operating systems are still in the experimental stage.

Operating system security induces a heavy system overhead penalty.

D. Major Types

The four major types of system software security are embedded in the system itself as executable code. They are:

1. Access licensing
2. Security logging
3. Secure kernels
4. Storage protection

These security measures are generally designed to be beyond reach of all but a few people, the system programmers. These people must ultimately be trusted, because they hold the keys to all system capabilities. Operating system (OS) software is the most critical component of security because of its control over the system and the user's need to trust it.

E. Objectives

1. Allow shared resource access—while fencing users rigorously from each other.
2. Restrict access of any system resource to the minimum needed to do the work.
3. Perform the minimum necessary functions exactly.

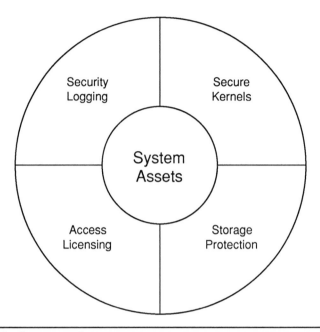

Figure 9.2. System software countermeasure types.

II. *Types of System Software Countermeasures*
(See Figure 9.2)

A. Access Licensing

1. *Definition*

Access licensing is the set of software procedures designed to authenticate the identity of valid system users and control their access to specific system resources.

2. *Implementation*

    a. *Identity/authentication tables.* Protected tables in the operating system which contain the set of valid user-IDs and the passwords or other information the user is to supply in order to authenticate his/her identity. May include both human and terminal hardware identifiers.

    b. *Authorization/access tables.* Protected tables in the operating system which contain the set of valid users (humans, terminals, and programs) and the system privileges granted to each. Privileges include any desired combination of users, terminals, programs, time of day, databases, data elements, sensitivity levels of input or output. The principle of LEAST PRIVILEGE applies.

c. *Secondary storage passwords.* In some systems it is possible to establish password control at subordinate levels of data within the file. An operating system table would implement this feature. The same general type of feature is available in CODASYL database management systems, which are discussed later.

B. Secure Kernels

1. Definition

Secure kernels are small, isolated portions of the operating system that perform the system's basic operations in a provably correct manner. This concentrates the key system protection mechanism (process creation and execution, and mediation of primary interrupts and responses) into a totally reliable segment of the system, rather than dispersing them throughout the software. Secure operating systems can then be built around these kernels.

2. Implementation techniques

a. Only a few experimental secure kernels have actually been constructed.

b. Primitive operating system code instructions (e.g., basic I/O and access licensing functions) are reduced to the smallest number feasible.

c. Instructions are converted via symbolic logic into a set of mathematical theorems that are the formal definition of the kernel code.

d. Theorem-proving programs are used to determine the validity of the instructions (to do exactly what they are intended to do, no more and no less).

e. If the theorems have formally proven correct, then the kernel is said to be certified.

C. Security Log

1. Definition

A security log is a protected data file written under control of the operating system that collects information on security-related events that occur throughout the computer system. This includes such items as user log-ons, operator requests, times of occurrences, acceptances or denials of authentication, accesses to sensitive data, etc. The log is used by security monitors to identify misuse of data or resources and system weaknesses.

2. Implementation

a. *Operator console activity.* Logs all requests or commands issued by the operator. May flag all privileged commands which allow console modification of programs or data in main memory or which affect secondary memory. Could also identify operator requeuing of output files for printing of multiple copies of sensitive reports.

b. *Terminal and batch user activity.* Logs all requests for user identification, and flags failures to authenticate correctly. Logs all requests for access to sensitive system resources, and flags all requests denied. Logs all important user activity while connected, to show programs run, files accessed, and actions taken.

c. *Real-time threat monitoring.* Logging of unusual activity may trigger real-time system security response when patterns indicate potential threat. Responses may include audible alarms at security stations, automatic job termination, keyboard lockout, and similar protective activities.

D. Storage Protection

1. Definition

Storage protection is a general term for a number of actions taken by the operating system to prevent unauthorized access to data by confining an application system to authorized storage areas and initially empty work areas.

2. Implementation

a. Automatic write-over of released files and work areas in both primary and secondary storage. Prevents "scavenging" of residual data by succeeding programs designed to read out contents of work areas before use.

b. Software store and fetch protection. Software bounds control to recognize read/write violations beyond assigned storage areas.

III. Topic Review

1. Recall several accepted systems software countermeasures.
2. For some specific systems software countermeasures, describe the purpose, limitations, and give examples of each.

TOPIC 2 DATABASE SYSTEM COUNTERMEASURES

I. Guiding Principles

A. Purpose

Database systems countermeasures are intended to protect the data in DBMS from intentional or unintentional attack. DBMS present special security problems because of the potentially large number of users with varying rights to data manipulation. Additionally, the data elements may vary in sensitivity, requiring different levels of protection.

B. Characteristics

Database countermeasures protect the integrity of database contents by limiting access and maximizing recovery in the event of failure. They also provide a record of the way the database changes over time, and give an audit trail.

C. Limitations

To make a DBMS truly secure and reliable, the file structure and management must be made far more complex. Individual data fields and elements need to be assigned levels of sensitivity. Access rights (read, modify, delete) must be defined for each user of the system to the lowest data levels. Sophisticated backup systems have to be designed to capture the status or condition of the database at any point in time. These requirements are costly and time-consuming to implement. With a large number of users or databases subject to restructuring, the security schema and tables may become quickly outdated. Finally, not many DBMS are designed to permit extensive security of this type.

II. Types of Database Countermeasures

A. Database Reconstructability

1. Definition

Reconstructability refers to the methods available to return a database to its original condition following destruction or damage.

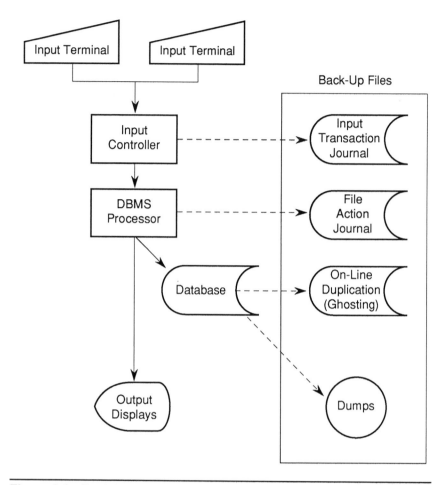

Figure 9.3. Real-time DBMS reconstruction countermeasures (Martin, 1976).

2. Implementation

    a. *Database save/dumps.* Dumps of the complete database to tape need to be made periodically. The frequency of dumping is dependent upon the data sensitivity in the database and its volatility (frequency and volume of changes applied). The tapes should be retained for several generations (grandfather, father, son) as needed.

    b. *Input/change transaction journals.* Between dumps of the database, all changes should be recorded on input transaction and file-action journal files. These files should also be dumped to tape periodically. If the database crashes, the previous dump tape can restore the old records, which are then updated with the contents of the transaction journal. The file-action journal will give a clear audit trail of the database changes for later study.

c. *On-line duplication (ghosting).* Very critical databases may warrant the dedication of additional on-line storage for continuous file duplication.

d. *Large database integrity.* Very large databases have two special problems: it takes a long time to copy or dump them, and many sections may have quite low volatility so that it may not be useful to dump them every time. A schedule should then be set up to dump portions of the file with a frequency that depends upon their volatility and importance.

B. Database Accessibility

1. Definition

DBMS may have their own access licensing. Other means may be used to render their contents tamper-proof, in addition to basic controls contained in the operating system.

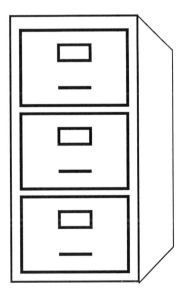

2. Implementation

a. *Sub-schema authorization control.* The CODASYL data description language permits attachment of "locks" to each data type in the scheme, down to data-item level. Programs or users must provide the "key" before gaining access to the data. Locks may relate to specific functions to be performed, which include reading the item, changing it, or inserting new items of that level. Other non-CODASYL DBMS permit varying degrees of embedded access control. An example is the SENSEG statement in IMS/VS, as when used in secondary indexing. This effectively limits the portions of the database available to an application.

b. *Encryption of stored data.* It is possible to scramble key portions of the database contents so that they are not readable to an unauthorized user. This technique has not yet been implemented widely. One example of the technique is the use of the "data compression edit" routine in IMS/VS, which permits exit/re-entry into a user-designed program for algorithmic data transformation if desired. However, this routine has a very high system overhead, which increases fetch and store times appreciably. It also must be loaded directly into the IMS and this could bring the whole system down in the event of an error.

C. Database Auditability

1. Definition

The broad accessibility of databases to both reading and modification makes it difficult to keep a record of changes.

2. Implementation

a. *File-action journal.* An on-line journal may be kept as part of the DBMS to record selected information about each transaction against the database. This permits the changes to be traced to a source.

b. *Journal analysis.* The contents of the file-action journal can be analyzed via program to show information on database use patterns and procedural violations that may be security problems.

D. Data Validity

1. Definition

The contents of the database must be protected against inadvertent errors and tampering. Countermeasures which address these

Types:

1. **Complete Files**	**File A**	**Record 1**
2. **Specific Records Segments**		**Record 2**
3. **Record Categories**		**Record 3**
4. **Data Item Types**		
5. **Specific Data Item Types**		
6. **Specific Data Items**		

Control Over Read

    Modify

    Delete

Figure 9.4. Subschema authorization control. Example: CODASYL privacy locks.

threats improve the validity of the database. Tampering with data may be malicious or fraudulent in intent.

2. Implementation (examples)

    a. *Statistical edits.* By performing statistical analysis on a database, the relationships between data elements can be uncovered in terms of distributions and ranges. Periodic re-analysis can isolate groups of data elements which fall outside of expected ranges and should be researched for validity.

    b. *Confederate data.* Data files and records may be inserted into databases for the sole purpose of determining whether the database has been tampered with. These records are never updated or changed in programs, but their values are periodically checked. If any change is observed, the database is considered compromised, and the file-action journals are researched for the cause.

User	Password	Data Elements	Transaction Types	Etc.

Any Combination of:

- User
- Database/Segment/Item
- Transaction Type (Read/Modify/Write)
- Terminal ID
- Time of Day
- Program
- Other Desired Factors

Figure 9.5. Subschema authorization control. Example: User authorization schemes.

III. Topic Review

1. Recall several accepted database system countermeasures.
2. For some specific database systems countermeasures, describe the purpose, limitations, and give examples of each.

TOPIC 3 APPLICATION SOFTWARE COUNTERMEASURES

The next type of CSS security to be described relates to application systems. This security is generally at a lower level than the two previously discussed. However, almost any type of software security can be implemented in application software if desired.

The objectives of application security are to design systems which are highly reliable and which will prevent erroneous data entry.

Application security is part of the system development process—controls are designed into the system, and they are integral to the logical system flow. As system design implies that risks have been identified, other types of security features are recommended as appropriate.

I. Guiding Principles

A. Purpose

Application software countermeasures are intended to create and maintain systems which are highly reliable and which prevent the entry of erroneous data.

B. Characteristics

They are part of the development process and the logical flow of the system. Secure application software is (by definition) clear and well documented.

C. Limitations

Application software countermeasures are ineffective in providing system security unless the operating system, hardware, and communications are secure.

Secure application systems are very straightforward in design, reducing programmer opportunity to use "creative" and esoteric methods.

II. Types of Application Software Countermeasures

A. Developmental Tools

1. Definition

Developmental tools are methods used during the system development process that help create secure application systems.

2. Implementation

    a. *Programming psychology (egoless programming).* The use of techniques such as the chief programmer team concept exposes the design and code to formal evaluation and scrutiny. This is valuable in reducing the more obvious security bugs and in discouraging complicated or fraudulent code.

b. *Structured programming.* The flow of control through a program is easier to follow and more understandable when structured programming and structured walk-through techniques are used.
c. *Structured system design (modularity).* This technique forces designers to be more logical in laying out program modules, in specifying clearly defined interfaces, and in passage of variables between the modules.
d. *Design standards and procedures.* A set of security-oriented standards for routine use of countermeasure techniques in the design process is essential. These standards are generally developed by the company with the specific operating environment in mind, so that the application system countermeasures will dovetail with other levels of security barriers.

B. Program Library and Change Control Procedures

1. Definition

A program library is a software package that automatically catalogs and controls program versions to ensure that only the correct version is used for production runs. Change control procedures are used to implement the features of the package for security purposes.

2. Implementation

a. Examples are proprietary packages and "PANVALET" and "LIBRARIAN."
b. Package permits storage and use of developmental programs for test purposes without disturbing production programs.
c. Permits the requirement of special authorization to change production program versions to avoid tampering.
d. May permit encrypted storage of production versions for further protection.

C. Data Editing Principles

1. Definition

System design for reliability and integrity includes built-in comprehensive data edits. These amount to qualitative and quantitative controls over the input data. Good data edits can make entry of fraudulent or erroneous transactions difficult. They can guard against the effect of poor communications between terminals and the system.

2. *Implementation*

    a. *Domain edits (value limits).* Data fields with known value ranges can be edited to ensure that input transactions conform to these ranges.

    b. *Control totals.* Blocks of input, as for payroll, can have key field totals calculated by the submitting office. The system can use these totals to verify the batch integrity.

    c. *Control fields.* Hash totals and checksums of selected fields or elements in records can be used to validate the integrity of the records as they are manipulated by the system.

D. Error Handling

1. *Definition*

Erroneous input records in sensitive systems need to be placed under control to make certain they are resubmitted correctly. This also helps trap and identify fraudulent or maliciously entered input transactions.

2. *Implementation*

    a. *Error logs and suspense files.* Sensitive data input records that have errors should be logged by the system for review. Suspense files should be periodically generated to show errors which have not been cleared or deleted by authorized users.

III. *Topic Review*

    1. Recall several accepted application software countermeasures.

    2. For some specific application software countermeasures, describe the purpose, limitations, and give examples of each.

TOPIC 4 HARDWARE COUNTERMEASURES

The next type of CSS security includes hardware. The main problem here is that most security features in this group must be designed into the equipment. Seldom can modifications be made to upgrade equipment security. However, without these features, the system does not have complete security.

I. *Guiding Principles*

A. Purpose

Hardware countermeasure techniques are part of the basic equipment architecture which are critical prerequisites for the construction

of secure operating systems. These features reduce the number of vulnerabilities that must be secured.

B. Characteristics

Hardware countermeasures are wired-in equipment features not affected by program code. They may be used by the operating system to intensify security. Some features are micro-coded on ROM (read-only-memory).

C. Limitations

These features generally are part of the original design and seldom can be retro-fitted.

Most hardware security features are not set up to operate without enabling instructions by the operating system.

II. Types of Hardware Countermeasures

A. Hardware State Variables and Instructions

1. Definition

Hardware architectural design that permits the system to operate in special secure processing states and restricts the execution of certain sensitive operations to these states.

2. *Implementation techniques*

    a. *Privileged/nonprivileged states.* Separate and distinct machine states of operation. In the privileged state, only the operating system is permitted to execute commands. In the non-privileged or "problem" state, application systems may execute commands.

    b. *Protected instructions.* A set of key control instructions that the hardware restricts for execution in the privileged state. Only the operating system may execute these commands, which control I/O, memory bounds settings, change of machine state, and other sensitive instructions.

    c. *Trap for illegal instructions.* Secure hardware will trap and abort all illegal instructions, such as unassigned opcodes, illegal combinations of legal opcodes and modifiers, and protected instructions being executed from the non-privileged state.

B. Memory and Partition Protection

1. *Definition*

Hardware designed for security has registers and other features which define the upper and lower bounds of memory or on-line storage allocated to a user or problem program. It may also provide for special lockout of memory or storage segments.

2. *Implementation*

    a. *Memory bounds protection.* Hardware capability to provide store and fetch protection by confining the problem program to certain bounds. This prevents unauthorized reading or modification of another user's programs or data.

    b. *Simultaneous access control.* Prevents access to data that is in modes which may allow unauthorized modification. For example, a file should not be accessible from the time a record is modified until control entries have been made on the master file and journal.

    c. *Storage locks and keys.* For sensitive blocks of memory, special protection keys may be established. This is a "lock" which prevents any I/O instruction from accessing the block unless the key is presented by the program. Any I/O instruction to such an area without the proper accompanying key would cause an interrupt to occur.

C. Other Hardware Countermeasures

1. Definition

A number of other countermeasures are being developed as the consumer demand for data security grows. A few examples of those available on some equipment are discussed here.

2. Implementation

  a. *Protected write-only activity logging.* Special circuitry which cannot be disabled or overridden by any program control that automatically collects information on selected system activities as they occur. Normally, this information is written out to a special disk or tape unit which is physically protected and is linked only to the logging circuitry.

  b. *Hardware monitors.* Hardware capability to monitor selected channel usage overtime to detect unauthorized use or theft of system service.

  c. *Hardware error checks.*

  d. *Emanations control.* All electronic equipment gives off electromagnetic signal emanations as it operates. Sophisticated eavesdroppers can use sensitive pickup devices to collect these signals and process them into intelligibility. In highly secure computer locations, the equipment may require emanations control, which consists of special techniques of shielding the devices cables and communications lines.

III. Topic Review

  1. Recall several accepted hardware countermeasures.

  2. For some specific hardware countermeasures, describe the purpose, limitations, and give examples of each.

TOPIC 5 COMMUNICATIONS AND TERMINAL COUNTERMEASURES

The final CSS security group includes those measures designed to prevent improper activity remote from the system itself. This whole area has now become extremely critical, as numerous criminals have discovered their ability to illegally access systems via ordinary telephone lines.

I. Guiding Principles

A. Purpose

Modern automated systems are based largely upon communications and terminal access. Databases, computer networks, and distributed processing are all oriented towards dial-up or direct line communications. Prior to this state of affairs, threats to the system were mainly physical. Now, the system threats may come from literally anywhere, with no need for any physical connection to the DPC or system. Communications and terminal system countermeasures are aimed to counteract these threats.

B. Characteristics

Communications and terminal countermeasures are directed towards the following: physical protection (access) of wired-in terminals, authentication of users attempting to gain access to the system, restricting the ability of unauthorized users to read messages they have typed into (encryption), and using the operating system to control the activities of on-line users.

C. Limitations

As communications and terminal security is highly complex, it is mostly automated. The vulnerabilities remain, in the form of the human procedures needed to make the countermeasures operate.

Without full security in the human element, installed communications security may give a false sense of safety.

Further, it is often easier to use traditional methods, such as subversion of employees or theft of listings from users, than to tap into a communication system which has some security countermeasures installed. A major limitation of communications security is that it is not effective unless more traditional (nontechnical) security countermeasures are operating well.

II. Types of Communications and Terminal Countermeasures

A. Physical Terminal Control

1. Definition

Physical terminal control basically means the set of countermeasures that restrict access to a wired-in terminal or the information available through it.

2. Implementation techniques

a. *Emanations control.* Same as for hardware (see previous module). Some terminals are notorious for the amount of electromagnetic radiation they emit. This is not an important countermeasure unless extremely sensitive or valuable information is being processed.

b. *Physical access.* Properly a physical countermeasure, but important to stress. Terminals directly connected to the system (as opposed to dial-up) may have broader system access rights than other terminals. They should be given greater physical security, so that access to them is tightly controlled. This may include key-lockable keyboard, locked doors, direct observation, etc.

c. *Limited-function terminals.* It is feasible to combine hardware and software countermeasures to restrict the function of a terminal to any desired level or type. An example would be strict data entry with no output capabilities or strict read-only with no input capabilities. These may be appropriate for sensitive systems or certain work areas.

d. *Hard-wiring of privileged terminals.* Special provisions are required for securing terminals that have privileged control over the system. These include the system operator console and the system security console. The terminals must be hard-wired in via both software and hardware techniques so that their addresses are not program changeable or interceptible.

B. Terminal Authentication Control

1. Definition

Methods which positively identify terminals, users, and messages to the system are grouped together under terminal authentication.

2. Implementation techniques

a. *Terminal device signature identification.* Terminals and other remote devices can be given capability of transmitting a unique identifier signal to the system upon query. This helps overcome the threat of an illicit user signing on to the system through a terminal not recognized by the system as having access license.

b. *Automatic call-back.* Terminals which have unique dial-up telephone numbers can be authenticated by means of call-back. The terminal dials up the system, is recognized by one or more authentication means, and both terminal and system hang up. Then the system automatically initiates a call-back to the terminal at the authorized number and reconnects.

c. *Security-conscious terminals.* "Smart" microprogrammable terminals are capable of authenticating a user even before connection to the main system. A number of methods are possible, including passwords or algorithmic responses, magnetic striped cards to be inserted into the terminal while the user is active, time of day accessibility, etc.

d. *Passwords.* This is a broad area which encompasses the use, generation, and protection of authenticating strings of characters known only to the system and a specific user. The basic concept behind password usage is that the system must authenticate a user's claim to identity in some way that is unique. However, password protection is only as good as the procedures used to guard the passwords from unauthorized discovery.

Password types: Random strings of characters: personal history identifier (e.g., "What is your mother's maiden name?"); simple algorithms (multiply the number shown on the string by the numeric sum of your initials and divide by your age); one-time keywords.

Password print suppression: The system must be designed so that passwords are not printed out on the terminal when entered, or are obscured by automatic overprinting as entered.

Password generation: Procedures or software to generate unique passwords should ensure that they are difficult to guess or determine programmatically.

Password life: Depending upon system sensitivity and user access levels, passwords should be changed periodically on the assumption that they will become compromised in use.

e. *Message authentication.* It is possible for a wiretapper to intercept and record a legal message and play it into the system at a later time. The use of time-dependent message authenticators will rule out the success of this maneuver. The time of transmission in an encoded form can be made a part of the message for system verification.

C. Encryption of Data Links

1. Definition

Encryption in general is the transformation of data in such a way that it is readable only to those in possession of the equipment (or algorithms) and keys by which it can be re-transformed or decrypted back to the original form. Encryption is intended to prevent accidental or intentional disclosure of data to unauthorized persons. Since encrypted data may be subjected to mathematical attack in order to uncover the key or algorithm, extremely complex methods must be used to increase resistance. The large volume of data to be encrypted increases the problem, since the more encrypted text available for analysis, the easier the solution may be.

2. Implementation techniques

    a. *Data Encryption Standard (DES).* Encryption of a highly sophisticated nature is now available commercially in the form of IC-chip devices containing the Federal Data Encryption Standard (DES). This code is breakable only in theory at present, because of the large expenditure of time and computer resources needed to uncover a single key, of which there are 2 to the 54th power (18 followed by 15 zeros) possibilities. DES devices may be used in almost any communications link to protect highly sensitive data. The DES, however, is not approved for use with national security (classified) information. Other National Security Agency (NSA) approved encryption devices must be used for this purpose.

    b. *Public-key encryption.* An alternative to DES is a technique that permits the encryption key to be known publicly, while the decryption key is known only to the recipient. This is based upon the work of two mathematical scientists, Diffie and Hellman, having to do with the difficulty of factoring out the product of very large prime numbers. The advantages are obvious, when one considers the serious administrative security problem of controlling the use and distribution of keys to users in an ordinary crypto system. The technique has not yet been widely adopted.

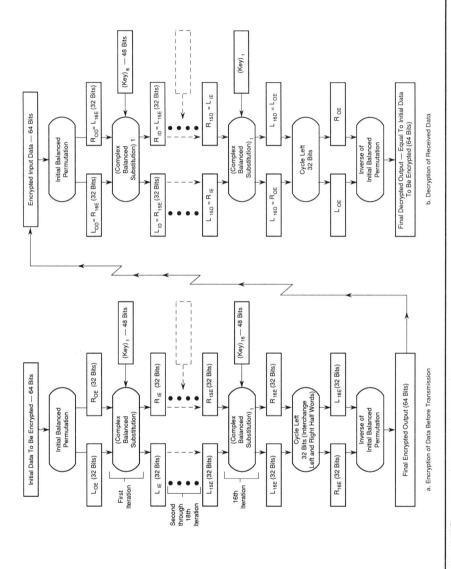

Figure 9.6. DES encryption and decryption.

125

1. Drop-In Device

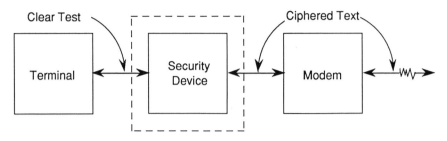

2. In-Built In Terminal

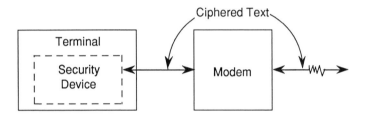

3. In-Built In Modem

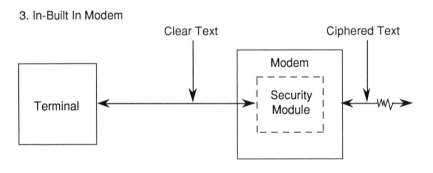

Figure 9.7. Various methods of implementing DES in data communications network.

c. *Privately-developed encryption equipment and algorithms for transformation.* The whole area of encryption is extremely esoteric in concept, relying heavily on the work of advanced theoretical mathematicians. Numerous schemes which appear highly sophisticated have been shown to be surprisingly vulnerable to attack by expert cryptanalysts. It is strongly recommended, by most knowledgeable experts in the field, that laymen NOT attempt to design their own cryptographic techniques for this reason.

d. *Cryptographic key control.* Every encryption system relies on the use of keys, or "arming parameters," which, when inserted in the encryption device or algorithm, cause a unique set of transformations of data to occur. It must be assumed for security reasons that these keys will be discovered if used for a certain length of time.

A general rule is that encrypted links in active use should change keys every 24 hours in a synchronized way. Keys must be generated in as near a random process as possible, and they must be tightly restricted in access and in transportation between users. Encryption devices should be designed so that the key is erased when the devices are opened for any reason.

D. Operating System Communications Control

1. Definition

The operating system can be used effectively to control access via communications. In addition to those countermeasures discussed in the module on the operating system itself, several techniques may be implemented that deal specifically with communications and terminals. Some of these are discussed below.

2. Implementation techniques

a. *Automatic terminal log-off.* Software to provide automatic log-off of a terminal that has been idle for a specified time interval. The length of time should vary with the type of system in operation and the terminal access controls being used.

b. *Off-hour terminal disconnect.* To prevent surreptitious use of terminals after normal working hours, the system should be set to cut off access rights to all but essential personnel.

c. *System masquerade control.* Software to prevent a user from issuing system-like prompts to another user terminal. This will ensure that users are not able to obtain sensitive identification information from other users.

d. *Terminal lockout (cease polling).* When a user has seriously violated security procedures, such as giving erroneous passwords or failing other tests, the system should be able to automatically lock the terminal out. The lockout may be for a specified period of time or until cleared by a security officer.

e. *Random re-authentication.* The system can request the user or terminal to re-authenticate identity at random intervals to prevent "piggybacking" of an illegal user on the line.

III. *Topic Review*

1. Recall several accepted communications countermeasures.
2. For some specific communications countermeasures, describe the purpose, limitations, and give examples of each.

10

Personal Computer Security

Companies are now realizing that personal computers or micro-computers, and the applications they are used for, are taking center stage in business. The information on PCs can include company strategic plans, pricing information, specifications, cash flow, and personnel and customer vital data.

Many of the users of PCs have yet to realize the value to the company of the information the PCs contain. Many have failed to back up their data, test the applications they write, or write documentation for their programs so that future users can understand them.

This chapter will deal with the users themselves and how their managers can protect what one firm called its "intellectual investment" in PC applications. In addition, it contains an outline guide to personal computer security as the last topic.

TOPIC 1 PERSONAL COMPUTER SECURITY OVERVIEW

The informal atmosphere of distributed data processing creates special security problems and requires a high level of user awareness and participation to protect the corporate data assets which are processed on microcomputers.

The special risks inherent in the use of microcomputers for business activities must be addressed at the corporate level. Users must become educated as to the substance of the risks, the means prescribed by management to reduce those risks, and the user community's role in the microcomputer data security function.

Some of the special security considerations associated with the proliferation of personal computers are:

- Protecting corporate informational assets by guarding against theft and/or corruption of easy-to-move and widely accessible hardware and perimeters at multiple sites.
- Consistency and synchronization of databases where multiple copies exist and access is harder to control.
- Communications problems specific to microcomputers.
- Library protections such as file backup, sufficient documentation, and contingency planning in an environment of decentralized operations.

The nature of distributive data processing, i.e., widespread use of microcomputers, places most of the burden of data security responsibility on the users of those microcomputers. The owner/user of the microcomputer must become familiar with the security risks inherent in the microcomputer environment and with the methods and practices used in combating those risks.

Security is a managerial rather than a technical issue. It is the responsibility of local management to access, monitor, and coordinate the security efforts of its staff. Local supervision is the keystone of PC data security.

The company MIS data security group should be concerned with the education of the personal computer user community in the areas of microcomputer security issues, and it should be instrumental in raising the awareness level throughout the corporation. In addition, the data security group should take an active role in formulating corporate PC data security policy.

TOPIC 2   FILE ENCRYPTION ON PERSONAL COMPUTERS

File encryption is a tool used to protect sensitive data which is stored or processed on microcomputers and related media. While it offers a special sort of protection, there are some serious drawbacks to encryption as a security measure which should be considered carefully before it is used. This topic is intended to inform users and management of the encryption option, with special attention to the security risks inherent in its use.

File encryption is the process of encoding a file according to a key supplied by the user and an algorithm supplied by the encryption product used. The original text of the file is scrambled into seemingly random data; it is unreadable until the same key is used to decode the file. The encryption process may be controlled by hardware or software. There are numerous products available for microcomputers.

Encryption is normally used to protect sensitive data. However, it has serious security drawbacks of its own, which should be carefully examined before any encryption system is implemented. The size of the file of data and the complexity of the algorithm used in the encryption process will have a direct effect on the processing time.

In a hardware-based system, where the encryption process may be driven by circuitry or chips, vulnerability exists in that the board containing the key may be stolen, lost, or damaged for use. This scenario contains two dangers. One is that all encrypted files are lost to their owner, as they cannot be decrypted without the hardware. The other is that the PC user may think new sensitive data is being encrypted when, in fact, it is not, thus leaving the data in readable form.

Software encryption packages rely on excellent key security. If the user loses or forgets the key, all encrypted data is lost. Conversely, anyone who discovers the key has immediate access to the data.

The user and management should work together, through risk analysis, to weigh the need for encryption and the risks and costs of additional security efforts associated with encryption as a tool. If it is decided that encryption is appropriate, the user and management should coordinate with the MIS data security group to choose a specific product. The next step is to implement the security practices and procedures necessary for safe and effective use of that product, e.g., preventing unauthorized access to boards in microcomputers.

TOPIC 3 SOFTWARE LICENSE AGREEMENTS

All PC users should be aware of their legal and moral obligations to adhere to contractual agreements with software vendors. Software developed outside of a company and purchased from a vendor will normally have a license agreement attached to it which imposes confidentiality requirements and possible use restrictions. Such an agreement is a legal contract and may contain restrictions concerning the use of software and copying of it for use on PCs in other areas. Typically, the software is patented or copyrighted and is to be used only on one CPU (i.e., computer). It may not be copied except for one archival (backup) copy.

Companies may want to establish the following guidelines for PC users with regard to third-party software:

- Program diskettes (third-party software) will be used only on the PC for which they were purchased.
- Program diskettes will not be copied, except as permitted to hard disk and for archiving purposes as allowed under the agreement.

Companies and their employees should be committed to honoring licensing agreements with software vendors and should oppose or prohibit the practice of software "pirating." Users needing software are expected to procure it through the procedures established by company policies. Individual users should be responsible for software they receive to run on the personal computers assigned to them. Diskettes containing outside vendor software should not be copied or lent to other users. When not in use, the diskette should be stored in a locked cabinet or other secure place. Library audits should be periodically performed.

TOPIC 4 PERSONAL COMPUTER CONTINGENCY RECOVERY PLANS

Contingency plans should be formulated for personal computers used to process corporate data. In order to adequately protect corporate informational assets, attention must be given to recovery plans to be implemented in the case of an event which interrupts processing on microcomputers.

Recovery plans for a disaster which could affect or halt data processing on microcomputers entail three elements:

A. Offsite Storage of Software Copy

Backups created on a regular basis should be stored "offsite." In the microcomputer world, offsite may be defined as on a floor other than where the PC and working versions of the software reside. The idea behind an offsite storage facility is to prevent the destruction of every copy of the software in case of a disaster such as a fire or a flood. Obviously, an effective backup strategy is essential to any meaningful offsite storage arrangement.

B. Good Documentation of Software Systems

Applications should be well documented. Documentation should include the following information:

1. A description of the overall purpose and objective of the application.
2. Data description of each file, showing fields and field lengths, and what the data is. Examples are helpful.
3. Process description—what programming language and/or software package was used to develop the application, and what happens to data during processing.
4. Descriptions of output documents such as screens or printouts, and a list of who receives any reports. Sample reports may be of value.
5. User procedures should be written up to tell how the system is used, how data is input, and what steps are performed to complete processing.

C. Arrangements for an Alternate Processing Site

Users may wish to make arrangements for use of a compatible system in case their own PCs are destroyed or stolen. A good rule of thumb is whether one can continue to perform his or her job for two weeks without the PC, as it will typically take at least that long to replace it.

Planning for recovery for PC users requires organization and cooperation within the user community. Users should formulate and test contingency plans before the fact. Software backup should be done on a regular and fairly frequent basis (probably at least weekly). If the developer of an application is not the primary user, documentation should be a joint effort.

Each user must weigh the consequences of the loss or destruction of the software and hardware for which he or she is responsible, and make recovery plans appropriate to the impact of such loss.

Management is responsible for appraising, implementing, and supervising contingency plans on a local level. Testing of different aspects of a recovery scheme should be conducted intermittently in order to identify and correct problems in the plan.

TOPIC 5 PERSONAL COMPUTER BACKUP PROCEDURES

The PC users should establish a routine of regular and systematic backup of micro files. The systematic storage of backup diskettes containing software and data files is an essential ingredient of computer security and must be carefully thought out. File backup protects the user and the operation of his or her system in the event of destruction of data by a disaster such as fire, theft, malfunction of a PC, or power surge.

Some backup of micro files is necessary on all microcomputers, but the frequency and amount of information saved must be determined on an individual system basis by the PC user and/or owner.

Frequency of backup should be determined based on the following factors:

- Importance of data to the business function
- Effect of loss of data to other systems
- The rate at which data accumulates
- The frequency of changes to the data
- The rate of deletion of data
- The difficulty involved in reconstructing the data

In some instances, the logistics of the backup process may warrant partial backups, that is, selectively choosing which data is to be duplicated. This is determined by the value to the company associated with that data or how critical it is.

The medium to be backed up is also a factor in formulating backup routines. For systems which use diskettes exclusively, daily or weekly backup may be appropriate. For hard disk systems, however, it is usually impractical to back up on a daily basis, as it requires approximately 28 diskettes and three or four hours to back up a typical 10-megabyte fixed disk. Selective backup may be the most desirable option for the hard disk system.

All backup diskettes should be clearly labeled to list the contents, date of backup, and the format of the information. Backup strategies should include some offsite storage, possibly through a reciprocal arrangement with a department or group on a different floor. The user may wish to keep one backup copy for his or her own use and send another to the offsite storage repository.

The method and frequency of microcomputer file backup must be determined by each user, based on the storage media and the volatility of the data involved.

It is imperative that management become involved in formulating backup procedures on a group or departmental level and in negotiating reciprocal arrangements for offsite storage and backup processing locations.

TOPIC 6   MICRO-TO-MAINFRAME CONNECTIONS

Data security strategies for controlling the process, techniques, and practices by which stand alone microcomputers are linked to mainframes should be included in a corporate security procedure. The purpose of linking microcomputers to mainframes is to allow the performing of functions that are unavailable within the processing capabilities or informational domain of the stand alone PC.

The micro–mainframe link should meet the following security criteria in order to be favorable to corporate interests:

- Access must be obtained on an authorized basis only.
- Connectivity must be delimited and managed.
- Threats to mainframe data integrity must be minimized.
- The potential for destruction of data must be curtailed as far as possible.

While the advent of the micro–mainframe connection has made quick retrieval of business information a proficient tool for daily operations throughout the corporation, management has had to address the new security problems which arise as a result of these links. Policies and procedures needed to manage the new relationship between PCs and host computers should be studied and assessed. The basic thrust of control strategy in this area must concentrate on protecting the mainframe and its databases.

There are three types of access to mainframe computers available to users. These are referred to as dumb terminal emulation, intelligent terminal emulation, and integrated processing.

A. Dumb Terminal Emulation

Dumb terminal emulation means that the PC functions just like any terminal connected to the mainframe computer. It has terminal access on a screen basis and no files are downloaded to the PC's memory.

A user must apply to the telecommunications department for the hardware necessary for such a connection. In addition, if the user does not have a user identification on the host system, this identification must be requested through the data security group for access to the specific resources.

B. Intelligent Terminal Emulation

Intelligent terminal emulation allows the user to download files from the mainframe computer to the microcomputer, and, in some cases, to upload data from the PC to the host.

There are many risks to the integrity of the host database in an environment where users can alter the data. Not only is deliberate sabotage a danger, but entry errors and local processing errors add to the risk of damage to the data, making the integrity questionable. There exists the possibility of two users simultaneously working with copies of the same host data and updating the host files at cross purposes. These are serious problems associated with intelligent terminal emulation. Even in a download-only situation, once the data is at the PC, no guarantees can be made for its accuracy. Not only may it become quickly outdated, it may be modified on a local level (i.e., at the PC) and no longer be valid.

The linkage software in use is authorized by a local administrator. Users are given various levels of access to data as approved by management. While some monitoring is performed by the software package, the most serious threats to mainframe data are beyond the scope of software packages currently on the market.

C. Integrated Processing

Integrated processing allows the users to do some processing on the mainframe, selecting and sorting data into a form usable on the PC, before storing it on the PC.

As with all PC security, the ultimate responsibility falls on the individual user and local management, with interfaces with the systems department and communications department.

TOPIC 7 PHYSICAL SECURITY IN THE PC ENVIRONMENT

The protection of hardware, supplies, software, and data is the duty of the PC owner or user and the local management. PC security is based on user awareness and participation. Corporate guidelines should be established to help the PC user community safeguard microcomputer hardware and assets against a variety of threats.

Physical security issues in the microcomputer environment are basically the same as those associated with mainframe computers. They are concerned with protection against theft, sabotage, accidental damage or destruction, and environmental hazards. The difference is that instead of concentrating security efforts around a centralized area, management must give its attention to establishing data security practices across the corporate PC user community.

A. Theft

The two main safeguards against theft of PCs and PC peripherals are:

1. Keeping a current inventory of all equipment and its location and responsible person
2. Securing that equipment

Distribution and inventory of microcomputer hardware should be handled by the telecommunications department. All PC components should be marked with a serial number, and records should be kept of where the equipment is located and who is responsible for it. PC software distribution and control should be under the user systems department.

There are several alternatives for protecting PCs not in a secured area. All microcomputers should be safeguarded with at least one of the following measures:

- Enclosures—heavy steel cabinets which are anchored to a desk or table. These cabinets enclose the entire PC and its peripherals, e.g., keyboard, printer, modem.
- Mounts—lockdown devices which fasten the PC to a desk or tabletop. The mount is used to make removal of the PC as difficult as possible, but the associated drawback is that the mount is virtually permanent and the user cannot ever move the PC.
- Cables—steel cables which run through loops attached to the PC and its peripherals. Although cables are a simple, inexpensive, and flexible method of securing a PC, they are not always the most effective as they may be relatively easy to cut.

- Alarms—alarms that sound if the PC is moved or the alarm itself is tampered with. Alarms serve as a deterrent only and do not prevent the removal of the PC.
- Keylock Access—devices which control the power switch on the PC and secure the rear of the PC, protecting boards. As with alarm systems, these devices provide limited protection on their own and should be used in conjunction with a method which prevents removal of equipment.

Users should not remove from the building PCs used at work.

B. Sabotage

The same methods of physically securing the microcomputer against theft will aid in preventing deliberate abuse/destruction of computer equipment. Another very important safeguard against sabotage is the storage of diskettes in a locked cabinet or drawer.

C. Accidental Damage

Most damage done to PCs and data is not deliberate, but the result of ignorance. All users should be properly trained to use the equipment and the software. Good documentation should be provided to the PC user, and additional training should be available if necessary.

D. Environmental Hazards

Aside from disasters on a large scale, such as fire or flood, microcomputer equipment is vulnerable to smaller threats.

The most prevalent of these smaller threats is the power surge, caused by electrical motors operating on the circuit, load shifting in the electric power, or lightning. Although a power surge may last only a fraction of a second, it can destroy equipment and data. Microcomputers should have a surge protector (sometimes called a spike protector) between the power source and the computer.

Another problem which may occur is heat buildup. This can be caused by using an enclosure to stack peripherals together that does not allow good ventilation, or even by adding peripherals, which causes the computer to work harder to drive them. Heat will eventually damage computer equipment. A small fan may reverse the effects of heating problems caused by poor circulation.

Static electricity can be a problem if the air is very dry. If static electricity is present at a high level, anti-static mats or carpets may be installed. A widely used solution is to mix a little fabric softener in a gallon of water and lightly spray the carpet once or twice a week.

Studies of microcomputer environments show that there is a general lack of awareness regarding information security. Management must lead the way to organizational awareness of the importance of security procedures.

The objective of data security is not just to protect classified information, but to ensure the confidentiality, availability, and integrity of the whole computer system.

Local management must take the initiative in assessing risks, formally assigning responsibility for information, providing adequate training, ensuring that the users in its area are knowledgeable of the vulnerabilities to their equipment and information, and establishing and monitoring consistent procedures.

The basic operational responsibility for information security belongs to those who own and use the information. Users must accept responsibility for protecting the sensitive and critical organizational data they handle through their microcomputers, and take sensible precautions to safeguard the microcomputers and storage media they use.

TOPIC 8 PERSONAL COMPUTER SECURITY OUTLINE

I. General

Sensitive and/or valuable information should be protected from accidental or unintentional modification, disclosure, or destruction, whether it is stored on mainframe, mini- or microcomputers, or on paper. *The level of security applied should be appropriate to the value of the information*, not necessarily to the value of hardware on which it is stored.

Types of security which should be considered are:

1. Physical security
2. Disaster recovery/contingency planning
3. Data security
4. Communications security
5. People and procedures

II. What Information Should Be Protected?

Categories of data which should be protected include:

1. Financial data
2. Proprietary data (example: trade secrets, competitive bids, customer lists)
3. Data which is subject to privacy restriction (example: personnel records, medical records)
4. Data which if tampered with could cause monetary losses (example: vendor names and addresses, accounts payable and receivable, inventory records)
5. Data which if destroyed could cause business interruptions for a unit or the company
6. Data which is costly to create, such as programs and databases

III. Special Characteristics of Personal Computers

Personal computers have some special characteristics which must be considered when deciding on security measures to employ. They include:

1. Price/availability—personal computers are relatively inexpensive and, therefore, are proliferating throughout the company.
2. Mobility—the hardware, software, data, and storage media are easily transported. Many divisions allow employees to take PCs home at night and on weekends. Diskettes are easy to conceal. Even if they are not concealed, it is doubtful that any security guard would question the presence of a diskette in someone's briefcase or pocket.
3. Poor separation of duties—in most instances the end user is all things to the PC. He or she is the programmer, the operator, the input clerk, and the user. Checks and balances are not easily designed.
4. Few controls in place—
   a. Change control—why were changes made? who authorized them? what were they?
   b. Few audit trails
   c. Little documentation
   d. Control of diskettes
5. Little planning for contingencies—many users have no backup for sensitive data and no recovery plans.
6. Mostly standard software packages—these software packages must be licensed for each machine on which they are used. If they are copied without the proper licensing, the company is liable to lawsuits.

7. Security features lacking—most of the popular software and hardware have no built-in security features. Vendors often discourage users from even asking about security features.

8. Data integrity concerns—the integrity of data stored on PCs, passed to PCs, and passed from PCs is a major concern. Because traditional checks and balances and separation of duties are not practical in the personal computer environment, other measures must be instituted. This is particularly important in cases where data is downloaded from a mainframe or mini to a PC, or uploaded from a PC to a mainframe.

   a. Data created and stored on PCs—because, in most cases, traditional checks and balances and separation of duties are not practical in the personal computer environment, other measures should be instituted to ensure that the information is valid. In most cases these will consist of manual checks and automated audit trails in conjunction with other security measures discussed above. It is imperative that management be aware of the data stored on its personal computers and how it is used.

   b. Data *downloaded* from mainframes or minis to personal computers, and data *uploaded* from personal computers to mainframes or minis—if the same files are used on both central computer systems and personal computers, extra care must be taken when changes are made. The file must be synchronized. If the files are not equal, information produced by either system will be doubted. In addition, there should be some central user approval of the distribution of the information from either system.

IV. *Types of Protections Available*

A. Physical Security

In general, the physical environment of an office area is sufficient for personal computers. Security guards and locked doors may be employed. In special instances other measures may be employed. Measures available include:

1. Anti-static mats and pads.
2. Terminal locks.
3. Power locks.

4. Specially designed cabinets with features which reduce the viewing area and can be locked.
5. Anchor pads—terminals can be anchored in place with special devices which require over 6,000 pounds of lift to remove.

B. Disaster Recovery/Contingency Planning

1. Hardware

Most personal computer hardware is easily replaced. Lead times are small or nonexistent. Elaborate plans are not necessary.

2. Software

Each user should analyze his or her needs in the software area. In most cases packaged software can be easily replaced. Custom software, if not easily recreated, should be copied onto movable media and stored separately from the computer. At the very least, listings of custom software should be stored separately.

3. Data

All users should have plans in place to recover data which has been destroyed. There are two ways of doing this: either rekey all the data or copy the data onto movable media and store it separately from the computer.

C. Data and Software Security

There are many methods available to protect data from unauthorized disclosure, modification, or destruction. The methods applied to any information should be consistent with the value of the information. Measures which should be considered include:

1. Access control

Access to the data stored on a personal computer may be controlled by any of the following:

    a. Access control software—software is available for many PCs which requires a user identification code and passwords. Audit trails are also provided.

    b. Terminal or power locks—these may be employed with only authorized users having keys. However, it should be noted that if an authorized user leaves the computer on, passersby could use the system.

    c. Locked rooms or cabinets.

2. *Encryption*

Data may be encrypted and made accessible to only authorized users. Encryption may be done in either software or hardware. The major advantage of encryption is that if a diskette is stolen, it cannot be read on another PC.

a. Hardware—boards are available which will encrypt data stored on the PC. The main disadvantage to encrypting the hardware is that the board could be removed. Removal of the board would not allow access to already encrypted data. However, the system could be used and the user might not notice that the board was gone, thus not encrypting sensitive data.

b. Software—Several software packages are available for the most popular PCs which offer encryption services. Most of the packages use the DES standard.

3. *Diskette control*

Diskettes should be recognized as valuable property and should be controlled accordingly. When not in use, diskettes should be stored in a safe environment. Records should be kept of each diskette, what it contains, and where it is. Audits should be performed on a periodic basis. Ideally, diskettes which contain critical data should be encrypted and copies stored at another location.

4. *Backup*

Sensitive data should be copied and stored separately to prevent losses from accidental or unintentional destruction.

5. *Packaged software*

It should be corporate policy that all trademark and copyright laws are followed. This means that packaged software must not be copied or used on multiple machines. Checking licenses should be part of any audit of a department.

6. *Custom software*

Custom software should be afforded the same protection as is sensitive data.

D. Communications Security

The following methods are available to protect information which is in transit between any type of computer, or to protect unauthorized access to any computer via standard telephone lines:

1. Leased lines

Leased lines provide a measure of protection because they cannot be dialed. However, they are still vulnerable to other types of intrusion, such as tapping or eavesdropping.

2. Answerback devices

Answerback devices are used on dial-up lines. A user dials the device and identifies himself or herself. The device checks the identification, hangs up, and calls the user back at a preauthorized number.

In cases where a preauthorized number is not feasible, the user may enter a number and the device will keep a record of it.

3. Encryption

Many devices are available which will encrypt data transmitted over standard telephone lines. Encryption provides the highest level security for data transmissions.

E. People and Procedures

While the traditional method of separation of duties is not practical in a personal computer environment, there are many other methods which can be employed to ensure system and data integrity. They include:

1. Management awareness—managers must be responsible for the activities of their subordinates and for instituting appropriate controls in the personal computer environment.
2. Personnel backup—more than one person should understand the system, the data, and how to use it.
3. Documentation
4. Audit trails
5. Change control

V. Recommendations

A. General

Each personal computer system must be evaluated individually to determine the levels of security required. Security measures employed should be commensurate with the value of the information stored in the PC.

B. Specific

At a minimum, the following should be mandatory for all personal computer owners:

1. All systems with hard disks should be locked in some way. Locked offices, cabinets, or key locks may be employed.
2. Diskettes should be stored in locked cabinets when not in use.
3. Backup and recovery plans should be in place.
4. Managers should be required to review their systems for security compliance on a yearly basis.

VI. *Protecting Mainframes and Minicomputers from PCs*

A. The Threat

Personal computers are proliferating both in offices and homes. Some personal computer users make a game of trying to break into corporate computers. If they do, they can cause major damage. In addition, many PC owners belong to clubs. It has been shown that one successful attack is followed by many more.

B. Protective Measures

The most common protective measures employed to prevent unauthorized access to mainframe and minicomputer systems are:

1. Access control software requiring user identification codes and passwords
2. Encryption
3. Answerback devices
4. Employee awareness
5. Restrictions on or eliminating dial-up access
6. Leased lines

11

Computer Viruses

Introduction

A virus, as defined by *Webster's* dictionary, is an "organism causing disease; (a) corrupting influence."

More specifically, a virus is a form of *threat* (see Chapter 2) that when given an opportunity to enter your system can:

1. Cause damage to a part of the system or to the whole system.
2. Not do any damage but spread itself to other systems where damage may be done.
3. Reproduce itself in any system it enters.
4. Lie dormant and unnoticed for some time until activated in some manner.

A virus, as it relates to computers, can be defined simply as the existence of unplanned software code that is in your system with the intent of doing, or causing to be done, harm. Another way of putting it would be that a computer virus can infect your system so that it does not function in the manner intended.

Viruses tested recently in the United States by Compulit, an independent software testing organization, have produced the following symptoms:

- File allocation tables (which keep track of the specific locations on a disk of segments of programs and data files) were destroyed, causing the user to lose everything on the disk.
- Disk assignments were modified so that data was written to the wrong disk.
- Executable programs and data files were erased on hard disks and diskettes.
- Data files were modified and all file sizes were increased.
- The execution of RAM-resident programs was suppressed.
- Available free storage space was reduced by making extra copies of programs and data files.
- Volume labels were changed and directories wiped out.
- Systems were suspended so that they would not respond to keyboard entries.

TOPIC 1 TYPES OF VIRUSES

A. Properties of a Virus Program

When a virus program is given control, it will search the disk drive for a user program that can be modified for its use. Most viruses will check to see if the user program has been infected already. They do this by looking for some kind of identification in the program to see if the virus code has already been planted .

If not, then the virus program will turn "on" what is commonly known as a "marker byte" and proceed to infect the program. The marker byte can usually be found at the beginning of a program or at a particular offset into the program used by the virus. The infection can be right next to the marker byte (as is usual for program tables) or at one or more particular offsets into the program.

If, on the other hand, the program finds its marker byte turned on, it will usually skip over the program and continue the search for the next virgin program. This keeps the virus from reinfecting itself and also lessens its chance of being discovered.

When an infected user program is executed, the virus program is executed (because it has taken space with a virus kernel in the user program), thus causing the virus to spread and do damage.

B. Categories of Viruses

There are well over 200 known virus strains and substrains that attack PC systems, both IBM PC compatible and the Macintosh environment.

Viruses can be categorized as four different types:

1. The *"Trojan Horse" virus* gets its name from the Trojan Horse of Greece used during the battle for Troy in the 12th century, B.C. The Greeks built a huge wooden horse and inside hid their soldiers. When they pushed the horse to the gates of Troy, the Trojans thought it was a gift and brought it inside the city gates. At nightfall, the Greek soldiers dropped out of the horse and attacked the unknowing Trojans. In a computer, the Trojan Horse virus will do something that appears to be a gift—putting on some kind of display or playing music, etc. While the user continues to run the program, the virus can be infecting the system or reformatting the hard disk unnoticed. This type of virus may be found in production software.
2. *Logical viruses*, or logic bombs, are designed to go off on a specific time, date, or condition. The main characteristic of this type of virus is that it does not only modify its host program but deletes the host and takes its place through a simple renaming.
3. *Worms* are viruses that dig themselves into a computer's memory or hard drive and then alter data. A worm is a type of program that will reproduce itself by creating copies. It is also characterized by not needing a host program in order to reproduce. Worms may bury themselves through all levels of a computer system.
4. *Computer viruses* are called this because they have all the traits of the first three with one exception. This virus, once in the system, can spread from file to file, program to program, directory to directory, and/or system to system, which can cause damage throughout a PC network. This characteristic makes the computer virus the most serious type of virus threat to the business environment.

C. Viruses in the PC World

Computer viruses fall into two basic classes: benign and malicious. Benign viruses are annoying, but cause no serious damage. Malicious viruses destroy the integrity of the disk's contents. The following "war stories" describe examples of both classes.

The Lehigh Virus, which infected over 5,000 PCs, was discovered in late 1987 at Lehigh University in Bethlehem, Pennsylvania (not to be confused with E. Stroudsburg State, where my oldest son, John, is majoring in computer science). It was extremely malicious and not only damaged several hundred university diskettes and crashed the laboratory microcomputer's hard disk, but also infected innumerable diskettes owned by students and faculty members. This virus was spread by damaging the COMMAND.COM and then attaching the file allocation table (FAT) or by formatting the hard drive. The virus ran its life for almost a month before being detected. This is a good example of a *Trojan Horse virus*, and its source was not determined.

The Friday the 13th Virus was so named because of when it was identified and is a good example of a *logic bomb*. The virus was programmed to infect the .EXE or .COM files in any given program. It is copied from system floppies to the hard drive. Then it spans from a file to program files once the program is executed. Rebooting or powering down erases the infected files. Also, the virus expands the program's size to make it too large to run and thus of no use.

The IBM Christmas Tree Virus first appeared on IBM's internal communications network in December 1987. The prank program consisted of an innocuous tree. It duplicated itself many times over, filling the network with its clones.

The Brain Virus, alias the Pakistani Virus, is a good example of a *computer virus*. This virus is known to have destroyed important records and data at a newspaper, hospital, and several universities (Delaware, Georgetown, and Pittsburgh). The virus copied itself into all bootable disks inserted into the infected computer.

The Scores Virus is an infection known to the Macintosh computer world. The source is not known, but when the virus was given control, the program would crash causing loss of data in the system RAM area. It would then start processing nondata or try to find missing instructions.

A good example of a virus with substrains in the Macintosh world is the nVIR Virus. This virus has several substrains that have evolved over the years. It and the substrains have been known to infect the invisible desktop files on Mac disks. It has been said, however, that no Macintosh virus so far has been capable of inflicting as much damage as have the viruses in the IBM PC world.

The Internet Transmitted Virus is probably the largest computer viral attack ever recorded. The attack started on Wednesday evening, November 2, 1988. Among the victims were computer systems at M.I.T., the University of California at Berkeley, NASA's Ames Research Center in California's Silicon Valley, the Los Alamos National Laboratory in New Mexico, Johns Hopkins University, and Bell Labs in New Jersey and regional Bell holding companies.

The virus traveled via electronic mail over Internet, an unclassified research and development network used by institutes to share data. The virus quickly multiplied, devouring computer storage space and slowing unprotected systems to a halt. The virus did not wipe out data, but merely used up empty data storage space.

The nature of viruses indicate:

- The problem is a worldwide one, not restricted to the United States.
- With the data transmission capabilities now available, it is possible to transmit a virus around the world very quickly.
- Although some viruses are benign pranks, there is a growing tendency for them to be malicious.
- Viruses can involve a criminal element.

TOPIC 2 DETECTION OF A VIRUS

A. Recognizing a Virus

The only way to recognize if you have a virus in your system is to have a good systems programmer decipher the internal structure of the system to provide proof that a virus exists. However, this is probably not possible due to:

1. The size and complexity of the system.
2. The lack of a system trail of what it did.
3. The fact that by the time the programmer begins, the virus has usually done its damage and either left the system or is in hiding.

There are some clues that could indicate the presence of a virus:

1. Programs begin to run slower.
2. Programs perform disk access that they did not before.
3. Load time increases.
4. Vague system crashes happen.
5. Programs which could previously be loaded now will not run due to lack of memory.
6. Storage requirements of programs increase.
7. Unclear or unknown error messages appear.
8. Storage space on the disk decreases without files having been added or expanded.
9. Memory-resident software runs with errors or not at all.

These alone do not necessarily mean you have a virus, but they are worth looking into further.

B. System Crashes

The only objective of some viruses is to create errors in the system. From the S/360 days, this was a "system crash." Either the system just dies or it just sits there in a "wait state." Here, the system will not allow access from the outside, and there is no clue as to the cause of the error.

System crashes caused by viruses can have three sources:

1. Virus programs with their own programming errors
2. Incompatibilities with the system or the software installed on it
3. Intentional system crash

In most crashes, the system's warm start routines are also disabled, requiring the system to power down and then start from the beginning with a "cold start" procedure. A system crash does not mean a virus is present. In some cases, the cause could be power fluctuation, low-quality socket, a "cold" solder joint, or a bad computer chip. The point is that it may not always be a software problem, but could be hardware as well.

C. Viruses and Hardware

So far we have focused on viruses and their altering, destroying, or deleting of data and/or their making the system perform in a way other than as it was intended.

Now I will discuss, at least in theory, how a virus can cause damage or disruption of hardware devices. These can be described as "killer" programs.

There are three examples that come to mind.

1. A routine instructs the disk controller to place the read/write head of the disk drive on a nonexisting inner track. This can cause the head to jam against a stop on the inside of the drive.
2. Every S/360 programmer knows various "fun tricks" you can do in assembler language to peripheral devices (i.e., the printer, card reader, tape drive, etc.). The setting of the carriage control character can cause a 1401N01 printer to sail a box of paper. I just found a similar problem in my IBM PC with the printer and WordPerfect.™ The systems with a plotter will accept a com-

from the system to move the paper backward. If you backfeed a large number of pages, a printer jam will probably occur.

3. A program can also erase a control track from a hard disk. In theory, this will make the disk useless since it cannot be reformatted, not to mention the loss of the data.

4. A program can cause hardware damage indirectly by making the system do something repeatedly, such as numerous accesses to the hard disk, which will eventually wear it out. Another example is having the operating system move programs in and out of memory when no work is being done.

D. Viruses and Computer Time

The unauthorized use of computer time in dealing with a virus is seen by many as a minor problem, since viruses are small and don't run very long. In addition, the impact of the virus is hard to measure and the user doesn't know how long the virus has been in operation.

Inserting a virus to intentionally slow the system down cannot only cause theft of computer time, but will cause programs not to run because the system is too slow. The computer system will take the blame when in fact a computer virus is at fault.

TOPIC 3 COUNTERMEASURE STRATEGIES

Countermeasures taken to protect your system can be very costly when dealing with *software* to insure it is virus-free. The user must determine to what extent he or she wants to go for a virus-free environment. However, there are some procedures and controls the user can employ that are just good common sense.

A. Software

In the software arena, the only way to insure that your program is virus-free is to develop and program it yourself. The "self development" has some drawbacks associated with it, however. The first and foremost is that it requires a high degree of programming knowledge. In addition, you have to keep the program to yourself, possibly limiting its value.

The next step in degrees would be "employee development." The drawback in this case is the cost of an employee who has the programming knowledge. Checks along the development process must also be taken into account.

"Independent programmers" or programming for a particular client also has a drawback in that usually the contractors will not want to give the source code to the clients. They feel that since they created it, they have the rights to it for possible use in other areas.

"Software houses" are usually the most cost-effective means of obtaining custom software. The drawback may be that due to their size, the software houses have a stronger market power compared to an independent.

"Off-the-shelf software" provides the most cost-effective source of programming code. The problem herein is that you are purchasing something that had generic development objectives and, thus, you lose custom capabilities. This type of software is not adaptable, and the source is never provided to the user.

From a procedural point of view, two simple countermeasures can be taken to protect against virus infection.

1. Test all new software, regardless of source, on a stand alone system. This prevents a virus from spreading if the code is, indeed, infected. By all means, *do not* test it on a network.
2. Prohibit the use of "shareware" from computer bulletin boards. This is the major source of the spread of viruses in the world!

B. System Data

Countermeasures in dealing with the system *data* are needed to protect against manipulation or destruction of data files.

The first method is to engage the use of "protection software." This is the use of programs that report on unauthorized changes to the data or, in some cases, prevent changes from taking place.

"Monitoring" provides for periodic checking of data files. Examples include visual checks of small data files, verification software, and standard compare functions.

"Easily monitored data structures" are ones that are easily checked. These may take more memory, but are quicker and simpler to audit.

"Obscure data structures" have the advantage of being more complex in that the data modification virus will have to do more work to accomplish its objective. On the negative side, a change to a complex data structure may go unnoticed for a period of time.

"Encryption" is the most complex method to protect the data from attack by a virus. However, if the virus finds the "key," then your data is unprotected.

C. Removal

When a virus is found to have infected your system, the question remains as to how to get rid of it, or disinfect your system.

Recovering a system that has become infected with a virus will depend on:

- How much damage was done
- How long it was in your system
- How widespread the virus has become

Viruses may infect three different areas of a system. They are:

- Hard disk partition table
- DOS boot sector of a hard disk
- an executable file within the system

Here are some suggestions that are intended to aid in recovery and keep to a minimum the risk of further spread of a virus.

1. Power down the system. This will prevent any spread of the virus, and memory-resident viruses are also removed.
2. Disconnect all data transfer lines to prevent infections from propagating and viruses from entering the computer from the outside.
3. Boot from an uninfected "write-protected" floppy disk. Use the original version of the operating system. Execute the DOS SYS command to attempt an overwrite of the boot sector. If this doesn't work, then back up all data files and perform a low-level format of the disk.
4. Format all media that is not being used for recovery. This will destroy any virus residing on the media.
5. Check the backup data for consistency. If the most recent backup cannot be guaranteed, then the last copy that can be guaranteed must be used.
6. Install diagnostic or security software and check the system for any sign of a virus.

TOPIC 4 COMPUTER SECURITY SOFTWARE

A virus protection package with the ability to destroy or inoculate against the virus can be used if the virus is a known strain. Care should be taken to insure that when erasing the virus, data is not accidentally erased which was not corrupted by the virus.

A utility program can be used to write over ('xx' or hex 'FF') the program that contains the virus, providing another method of abolishing a virus. This allows the user to replace the damaged portion with an uninfected backup and eliminate accidental erasure of files.

There are also programs that can be placed in the AUTOEXEC.BAT to check the COMMAND.COM to see if the number of bytes has been modified.

Some of the security packages available will feature:

- Protection against unauthorized users
- Protection against viruses
- Disaster recovery
- Virus detection
- Data integrity protection
- Program access control

There are several security anti-virus software packages that can be obtained for the IBM PC or Macintosh environment. Some examples are:

- Certus 2.0, FoundationWare, Cleveland, OH
- Secure Wrap(PC), Commcrypt, Inc., Beltsville, MD
- Watchdog, Fischer International, Naples, FL

A utility that is very useful in dealing with viruses is VIRUSCAN, developed by McAfee Associates, 4423 Cheeney Street, Santa Clara, CA 95054. They are also the author of the "Virus Characteristics List" found at the end of this chapter.

VIRUSCAN scans diskettes or entire systems and identifies any preexisting PC virus infection. It will indicate the specific files or systems areas that are infected and will identify the virus strain which has caused the infection. Removal can then be done automatically with a system option of the utility. If the infection is widespread, automatic disinfector utilities are available which can remove the infected segment of files and repair and/or restore the infected programs.

Conclusion

A key to protecting against viruses, as seen by William Murray, an information and security consultant with Deloitte & Touche of Wilton, CT, is controlling *who* can execute a program. With the widespread implementation of local and wide area networks, systems are conducive to the spread of viruses are currently being implemented.

System security should have a three-pronged purpose:

- To protect against the physical removal of the PC
- To eliminate unauthorized data access
- To prevent unauthorized access to programs

Finally, there is no such thing as a "harmless" virus. *All* viruses corrupt the code of the host programs, and none enter your systems under invitation.

VIRUS CHARACTERISTICS LIST V.64
(Copyright 1989, McAfee Associates, 408-988-3832)

The following list outlines the critical characteristics of the known IBM PC and compatible virus strains identified by VIRUSCAN. Beginning with version 63 of the list, we are including the number of known varieties of each strain. This number is listed in parentheses beside the name of the strain. The total number of known viruses is summed at the end of the list.

Virus	Disinfector	Virus Uses Self-Encryption	Virus Remains Resident	Infects COMMAND.COM	Infects COM files	Infects EXE Files	Infects Overlay Files	Infects Floppy Diskette Boot	Infects Fixed Disk Boot Sector	Infects Fixed Disk Partition Table	Increase in Infected Program's Size	Damage
1008	CleanUp	x	x	x	x						1008	O,P,D,L
Stoned-II	MDISK		x					x		x	N/A	O,B,L
Taiwan3	CleanUp		x	x	x	x	x				2905	O,P,D,L
Armageddon	CleanUp		x	x	x						1079	O,P
1381	CleanUp				x	x					1381	O,P
Tiny	CleanUp			x	x						163	O,P
Subliminal	CleanUp		x	x	x						1496	O,P
Sorry	CleanUp		x	x	x						731	O,P
RedX	CleanUp			x	x						796	O,P
1024	CleanUp		x	x	x						1024	O,P
Joshi	MDISK		x					x	x	x	N/A	B,O,D
Microbes	MDISK		x					x	x		N/A	B,O,D
Print Screen	MDISK		x					x	x		N/A	B,O,D
Form	MDISK		x					x	x		N/A	B,O,D
June 13th	CleanUp	x			x						1201	O,P,D,L
5120 (2)	CleanUp			x	x	x	x				5120	O,P,D,L
Victor	CleanUp		x	x	x	x	x				2458	P,D,L
JoJo	CleanUp		x		x						1701	O,P
W-13 (2)	CleanUp		x								532	O,P
Slow	CleanUp	x	x		x	x	x				1721	O,P,L
Frere Jacques	CleanUp		x		x	x	x				1811	O,P

Virus	Disinfector	Virus Uses Self-Encryption	Virus Remains Resident	Infects COMMAND.COM	Infects COM files	Infects EXE Files	Infects Overlay Files	Infects Floppy Diskette Boot	Infects Fixed Disk Boot Sector	Infects Fixed Disk Partition Table	Increase in Infected Program's Size	Damage
Liberty	CleanUp		x	x	x	x	x				2862	O,P
Fish-6	CleanUp	x	x	x	x	x	x				3584	O,P,L
Shake	CleanUp		x		x						476	O,P
Murphy	CleanUp		x	x	x	x	x				1277	O,P
V800	CleanUp	x	x		x						none	O,P,L
Kennedy	CleanUp		x		x						308	O,P
Eight Tunes/1971	CleanUp		x		x	x	x				1971	O,P
Yankee Doodle-2	CleanUp				x	x					1961	O,P
June 16th	CleanUp			x	x						1726	F,O,P,L
XA1	CleanUp	x			x						1539	F,O,P,L
1392	CleanUp		x	x	x	x					1392	O,P,L
1210	CleanUp		x		x						1210	O,P,L
1720	CleanUp		x		x	x	x				1720	F,O,P,L
Saturday 14th	CleanUp		x		x	x	x				685	F,O,P,L
Korea (2)	MDISK							x	x		N/A	B,O
Vcomm (3)	CleanUp				x						1074	O,P,L
ItaVir	CleanUp				x						3880	O,P,L,B
Solano (2)	CleanUp		x		x						2000	O,P,L
V2000 (3)	CleanUp		x	x	x	x	x				2000	O,P,L
1554	SCAN/D		x	x	x	x					1554	O,P,L
512 (4)	SCAN/D		x	x	x						none	O,P,L
EDV (2)	MDISK		x					x	x	x	N/A	B,O
Joker	CleanUp		x	x	x							O,P
Icelandic-3	CleanUp		x			x					853	O,P
Virus-101	CleanUp	x	x	x	x	x	x	x	x		2560	P
1260	CleanUp	x			x						1260	P
Perfume (2)	CleanUp				x						765	P
Taiwan (2)	CleanUp				x						708	P
Chaos	MDISK		x					x	x		N/A	B,O,D,F
Virus-90	CleanUp		x		x						857	P
Oropax (3)	CleanUp		x		x						2773	P,O
4096 (2)	CleanUp	x	x	x	x	x					4096	D,O,P,L

Virus	Disinfector	Virus Uses Self-Encryption	Virus Remains Resident	Infects COMMAND.COM	Infects COM files	Infects EXE Files	Infects Overlay Files	Infects Floppy Diskette Boot	Infects Fixed Disk Boot Sector	Infects Fixed Disk Partition Table	Increase in Infected Program's Size	Damage
Devil's Dance	CleanUp		x		x						941	D,O,P,L
Amstrad (5)	CleanUp				x						847	P
Payday	CleanUp		x		x	x	x				1808	P
Datacrime II-B	CleanUp	x			x	x	x				1917	P,F
Sylvia/Holland	CleanUp				x						1332	P
Do-Nothing	CleanUp		x		x						608	P
Sunday (2)	CleanUp		x		x	x	x				1636	O,P
Lisbon (2)	CleanUp				x						648	P
Typo/Fumble	CleanUp		x		x						867	O,P
Dbase	CleanUp		x		x						1864	D,O,P
Ghost Boot Version	MDISK		x					x	x		N/A	B,O
Ghost COM Version	CleanUp				x						2351	B,P
New Jerusalem	CleanUp		x		x	x	x				1808	O,P
Alabama (2)	CleanUp		x			x					1560	O,P,L
Yankee Doodle (3)	CleanUp		x		x	x					2885	O,P
2930	CleanUp		x		x	x					2930	P
Ashar	CleanUp		x					x			N/A	B
AIDS (3)	CleanUp				x						Overwrites Program	
Disk Killer (2)	CleanUp		x					x	x		N/A	B,O,P,D,F
1536/Zero Bug	CleanUp		x		x						1536	O,P
MIX1	CleanUp		x			x					1618	O,P
Dark Avenger (2)	CleanUp		x	x	x	x	x				1800	O,P,L
3551/Syslock	CleanUp	x			x	x					3551	P,D
VACSINA (2)	CleanUp		x		x	x	x				1206	O,P
Ohio	MDISK		x					x			N/A	B
Typo (Boot Virus)	MDISK		x					x	x		N/A	O,B
Swap/Israeli Boot	MDISK		x					x			N/A	B
1514/Datacrime II	CleanUp	x			x	x					1514	P,F
Icelandic II	CleanUp		x			x					661	O,P
Pentagon	MDISK							x			N/A	B
3066/Traceback (2)	M-3066		x		x	x					3066	P
1168/Datacrime-B	CleanUp	x			x						1168	P,F

Virus	Disinfector	Virus Uses Self-Encryption	Virus Remains Resident	Infects COMMAND.COM	Infects COM files	Infects EXE Files	Infects Overlay Files	Infects Floppy Diskette Boot	Infects Fixed Disk Boot Sector	Infects Fixed Disk Partition Table	Increase in Infected Program's Size	Damage
Icelandic (2)	CleanUp		x			x					642	O,P
Saratoga	CleanUp		x			x					632	O,P
405	CleanUp				x							Overwrites Program
1704 Format	CleanUp	x	x		x						1704	O,P,F
Fu Manchu (2)	CleanUp		x		x	x	x				2086	O,P
1280/Datacrime (2)	CleanUp	x			x						1280	P,F
1701/Cascade	CleanUp	x	x		x						1701	O,P
1704/CASCADE-B (9)	CleanUp	x	x		x						1704	O,P
Stoned/Marijuana (2)	CleanUp		x					x		x	N/A	O,B,L
1704/CASCADE	CleanUp	x	x		x						1704	O,P
Ping Pong-B (2)	CleanUp		x					x	x		N/A	O,B
Den Zuk (3)	MDISK		x					x			N/A	O,B
Ping Pong (3)	CleanUp		x					x			N/A	O,B
Vienna-B	CleanUp				x						648	P
Lehigh	CleanUp		x	x							Overwrites	P,F
Vienna/648 (14)	M-VIENNA				x						648	P
Jerusalem-B	CleanUp		x		x	x	x				1808	O,P
Yale/Alameda (2)	CleanUp		x					x			N/A	B
Friday 13th COM	CleanUp				x						512	P
Jerusalem (9)	CleanUp		x		x	x	x				1808	O,P
SURIV03	CleanUp		x		x	x	x					O,P
SURIV02	CleanUp		x			x					1488	O,P
SURIV01	CleanUp		x		x						897	O,P
Pakistani Brain (3)	CleanUp		x					x			N/A	B

Total Known Viruses—182

Legend

Damage Fields: B–Corrupts or overwrites boot sector

O–Affects system run-time operation

P–Corrupts program or overlay files

D–Corrupts data files

F–Formats or erases all/part of disk

L–Directly or indirectly corrupts file linkage

Size Increase: The length, in bytes, by which an infected program or overlay file will increase

Characteristics: x = Yes

Disinfectors: SCAN/D   – VIRUSCAN with /D option
SCAN/D/A – VIRUSCAN with /D and /A options
MDISK/P   – MDISK with "P" option
All Others – The name of disinfecting program

Note: The SCAN /D option will overwrite and then delete the entire infected program. The program must then be replaced from the original program diskette. If you wish to try recovering an infected program, use the named disinfector if available.

12

Doing it Right

Introduction

This final chapter of the book is intended to tie together several of the concepts presented in the earlier chapters. It will describe in general how security measures can be selected and installed in a brand new application system as an integral part of the normal development process. You will see how good security is a basic function and outcome of standard methods for system definition and design.

I. Security and the System Development Method

A system's complete life cycle is divided into two *stages* as viewed by TSD (Total System Development method) developed by Frank G. Kirk of Illinois Bell.

The first stage is the *developmental stage*, the period from initial concept to installation of the new system. This includes:

- New application systems
- Major modifications to existing systems

The remainder of operational life of the system until phase-out or replacement is in the *maintenance stage*.

Let's examine these phases in more detail so that consideration of system security can be directed to specific developmental areas.

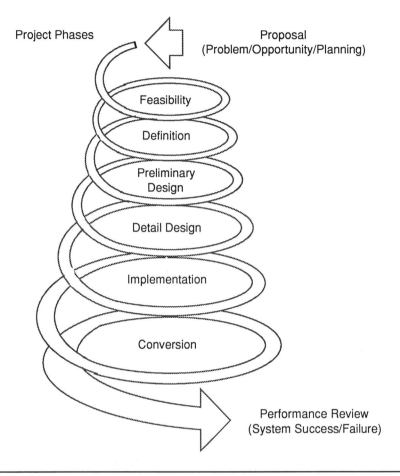

Figure 12.1. Total system development.

A. The "Phases" of System Development

TSD Development Stage is itself divided into eight phases. Each of these phases has a discrete and clearly defined set of key developmental activities.

Activities are expressed in terms of specifications for developmental documentation: if the documentation is fully completed, the developmental activity must have been done.

The phases are:

1. *Proposal*—identification by user of need for new system or major redesign.
2. *Feasibility*—analysis of proposal in terms of possible approaches, costs, and benefits.
3. *Definition*—detailed definition of information and functional requirements for system.
4. *Preliminary Design*—general architecture of system is designed.
5. *Detailed Design*—development of detailed procedural specifications for each component of system.
6. *Implementation*—construction and test of all system components, including programs and human procedures.
7. *Conversion*—installation and trial operational status of system.
8. *Performance Review*—final evaluation of development, performance, and effectiveness of system.

B. The Project Management (PM) Method

1. Method is geared directly to TSD phased approach, with set tasks to do during each phase.
2. Aids in specifying what needs to be done in managing a project and defining when each task needs to be done.
3. Basic components:
   a. Set overall strategy—results in project plan.
   b. Plan each TSD phase in advance. Activities: developmental, organizational, communications, procedures, control.
   c. Administer each phase—organize team's efforts, control activities to meet targets.
4. PM implies an interdisciplinary team—whatever skills are needed are brought on board for project. Some skills for security projects:
   a. Users
   b. Data systems—development and operations
   c. Auditing or quality control
   d. Data security administration
   e. Company security
5. Not all skills would be needed full time.
6. Note: Keep in mind that the developmental approach can be used for any major security implementation project, but the focus here is on a major application system under development.

II. The New System—Phases of Determining Security Requirements

A. The Feasibility Phase

1. Feasibility is the first active phase of a development project—analysis of user's proposal.
2. Identifies basic user needs for system. Key security items:
   - Data integrity and reliability—how sensitive is the system?
   - Access security—must system by "tight"?
   - Privacy implications—nature of personnel data in system.
3. Uncovers system's constraints—known problems that will affect design of system. Security items:
   - Legal or regulatory restrictions—e.g., FCPA control and auditability.
   - Company's competitive position—company secrets or significant dependency on system.
   - Technology available to team—may dictate choice of countermeasures, e.g., need to use IMS database with its cumbersome security.
4. Prioritized user security needs—outgrowth of preceding two points.
5. Preparation of alternative system models—different broadbrush approaches to system design.
6. Economic analysis of alternatives—very rough for security, as no specific measures can be established at that point.

B. System Definition Phase

1. Definition Phase establishes the expected performance criteria of new system—functional requirements.
2. Key phase for security—risk analysis tasks performed here.
3. *Potential Problem Areas*
   - Identifies areas inside and outside the system which could degrade product or performance.
   - Describes parts of system most vital to performance.
   - Identifies key critical dependencies between this system and others.
   - Describes other system problem areas.
4. *System Reliability Requirements*
   - Assesses potential impact of system failures (harmful events).
   - Estimates probability of each failure occurring.
   - Establishes requirements for system fallback and recovery.

5. *System Control Requirements*
   - Identifies critical system performance criteria needing control procedures.
   - Identifies activities required to ensure integrity of system data (e.g., accuracy, timeliness, completeness).
   - Establishes security requirements for data access, updating, and distribution.

III. The Phases of Creating a Secure System Design

A. Preliminary Design Phase

1. Phase of developing top-level system architecture—selecting types of countermeasures.
2. System security functions are allocated to:
   - Software programs
   - Hardware
   - Human procedures
   - Physical security

B. The Detail Design Phase

1. Phase of developing detailed specifications for system components—next step is program coding or personnel procedure writing.
2. Countermeasure specifications are treated identically to others for system.
3. Key security-related activities by functional area:
   - Program/software
   - Personnel procedures
   - Equipment and facilities
4. *System Controls Description*
   - Identifies all system control procedures designed to ensure system quality.
   - Describes the purpose or performance level to be attained by the control measure.
   - Brief description of corrective action triggered by the control.
5. *System Reliability Measures Description*
   - Identifies system features designed to ensure reliability and continuity.
   - Measures include: fallback, recovery, reconstruction, reconfiguration, data retention.
   - Procedures needed and guidelines for use.

IV. Phases for Implementing the Secure System

A. Activities in Implementation Phase

1. Actual program coding and procedure writing is done here.
2. Creation of control logic and PSS procedures:
   - Procedural control and reliability
   - Program logic control and reliability
3. Preparation of data center operating documents:
   - Scheduling and preprocessing requirements
   - I/O control and verification
   - Restart/recovery procedures
4. Security Testing:
   - Validation—logical correctness
   - Certification—operating performance
5. Preparation of preliminary guide on how to audit system activity.

B. The Conversion Phase

1. Phase of system installation in live environment and subsequent operational checkout.
2. Activities of phase:
   - Trail operation and evaluation of security measures
   - Checkout of audit guide
   - Revisions as required

V. System Security Maintenance

A. Performance Review Phase Activities

1. Performance Review is conducted three to 12 months after initial installation.
2. Designed to evaluate:
   - Conformance to design specifications
   - Meeting true user needs
   - Development efficiency

B. On-going Security Maintenance Program

1. Purpose is to ensure continued secure system operation.
2. Factors which may affect level of a system's security:
   - Change in sensitivity of data elements
   - Change in interfacing systems

- Modifications to programs or data elements
- Variations in enforcement of procedures
- Change in company's dependency on system
3. Security Surveillance Tasks:
- Periodic objective risk analysis
- Use of audit guide
- Test of back-up/recovery procedures

VI. *Topic Review*

1. Recall key aspects of the TSD method that should be applied to EDP security countermeasure implementation for an application system.
2. Recall the two phases of determining functional security requirements for an application system under development.
3. Describe the procedural steps in formulating and analyzing countermeasure design alternatives.
4. Review the three phases of implementing selected countermeasures in an application system.
5. Recall the two sets of functions which comprise the security maintenance and surveillance program.

Appendix **A**

Golden State Telephone Company Case Study

Table of Contents

The Golden State Telephone Co. Central Distribution Facility

1.0 Mission Description:

The Golden State Telephone Company serves about 3 million customers in a three state area. To support the various consumers of construction, maintenance, and repair material, the company maintains one central distribution warehouse. The warehouse facility is controlled by an onsite inventory control group that is responsible for all equipment purchasing, inventory storage, and distribution.

The Golden warehouse was "automated" in 1970 with the installation of a computer-based multi-function system to support all of the organization's major activities. The major system functions include:

- Material receipt and distribution. Record of all material received is entered into the system. This causes update of inventory records and automatic assignment of warehouse and bin locations. The system maintains records on current status of all inventory items. Requests for shipment are received via dedicated communications link from field repair offices or other material consumers and shipment "pick lists" and "Bills of Lading" are generated. The system manages the transportation to requestors by staging shipment to optimally use carriers, and planning the transportation schedules.
- Storage Management. Location and detail status of all inventory items is maintained. Quality inspection schedules are automatically planned based on equipment type and age of inventory, etc.

- Inventory control. An inventory planning group uses the automated inventory records and various inventory control models to maintain reorder levels, reorder quantities, etc.
- Procurement and contract administration. Procurement history records are maintained as well as detailed supplier and contractor information to support the purchasing group activities.
- The personnel and payroll system serves all employees in the organization.

2.0   *Facility Description:*

The Golden State Central warehouse is located on a 12 acre site on the outskirts of the largest city in the company's service area. There are 6 warehouses and an administration building. A central computer

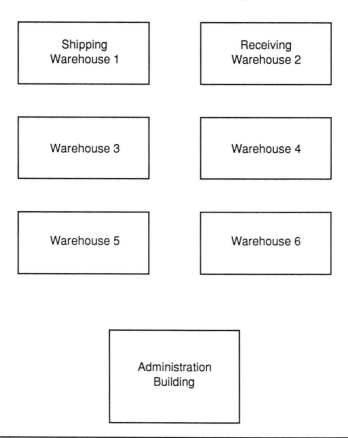

Golden State Distribution Center facility layout.

facility is in the basement of the administration building. Remote job entry stations are located in the personnel and finance areas, the inventory control group area, the material receiving area, and the shipping area. Every RJE station has 2–6 user terminals, and a high speed printer; some stations have a 9-track tape drive used to process output from key-to-tape unit.

At the central site, a third generation processor (fixed region multi-programming) is configured with 5 mag tape units, 2 high speed printers, a high speed card reader, 1.3 billion bytes of removable disk storage, and a communications front-end processor to support all RJE and local terminal access.

All terminals on the system can act as normal timeshare terminals with access to compilers, utilities, etc. All production systems run as on-line entry-retrieval systems or simple transaction systems where transactions are entered either in batch submissions or (for small volumes) one at a time via the terminals. In most cases, the application system serving a particular functional group will stay active on that group's terminal all day.

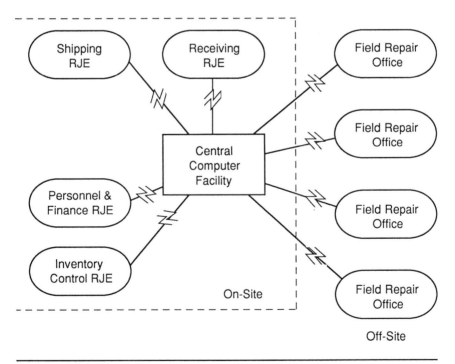

Golden State Distribution Center remote terminal configuration.

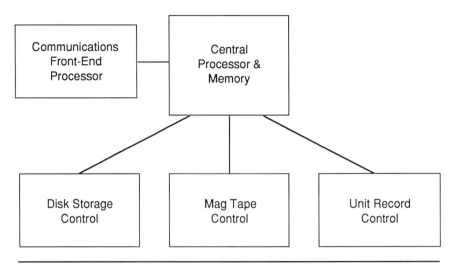

Golden State Distribution Center central computer facility configuration.

Access to terminals is controlled by a system password that is unique to each user. Access to individual application systems is controlled by the application programs.

Risk Management Program:

A risk management program was formally initiated in the summer of 1978. A security program was defined, and a data security administrator was appointed. In December 1978, a comprehensive risk analysis was completed. Portions of the documentation resulting from the risk analysis effort are shown on the pages that follow.

RISK ANALYSIS RESULTS OVERVIEW—RISK RATINGS BY FUNCTION CELL

(Functional Map of the Risk Survey)

	Input	Processing	Storage	Output
Material Distribution Inventory Control System	High	Med	Low	Med
Storage Management System	Low	Low	None	None
Procurement & Contract Administration System	Low	Med	Med	High
Personnel & Payroll System	Low	High	Med	Low

177

RISK SURVEY CHECKSHEET

(Indexes to Detail Descriptions)

Major Subsystem _____

Functional Cell _____

Vulnerability Areas

Threat Category		Data	Software	Hardware	Physical Plant	Media & Supplies	People	Commo	Other
Probabilistic	Natural Hazards								
	Equipment Failure								
	Human Error								
Algorithmic	Theft								
	Fraud								
	Malice								
	Strategic Attack								

Figure 9. Risk Survey Checksheet.

RISK ANALYSIS RESULTS OVERVIEW—RISK RATINGS BY FUNCTION CELL

(Functional Map of the Risk Survey)

	Input	Processing	Storage	Output
Material Distribution Inventory Control System	High	Med	Low	Med
Storage Management System	Low	Low	None	None
Procurement & Contract Administration System	Low	Med	Med	High
Personnel & Payroll System	Low	High	Med	Low

RISK SUMMARY CHART

Major Subsystem   INVENTORY

Functional Cell   INPUT

Threat Category	System Vulnerability Description	Harmful Event Description	Index #	Event Prob # Occ/Yr (Rating)	Impact $ Cost/Occ (Rating)	Risk Level (ALE) (Rating)
Fraud	Normal batch input process: Vulnerable to unauthorized transaction entry	Concealment of physical theft	1	2	2	2
	Remote terminals vulnerable to fraudulent use by unauthorized personnel from other areas	Initiation of unauthorized shipments	2	2	4	3
		Concealment of physical theft	3	3	3	3
		Unauthorized shipments	4	3	4	4
	Communications lines vulnerable to attachment of clandestine terminal	Concealment of extensive fraudulent operations	5	3	4	4
	Remote terminals are left unattended during some shifts	Concealment of physical theft or initiation of unauthorized shipments	6	3	4	4

RISK SUMMARY CHART

Major Subsystem INVENTORY

Functional Cell INPUT

Threat Category	System Vulnerability Description	Harmful Event Description	Index #	Event Prob # Occ/Yr (Rating)	Impact $ Cost/Occ (Rating)	Risk Level (ALE) (Rating)
Fraud	Operations personnel are vulnerable to coercion by outsiders	Persuasions of cleared operation personnel to enter fraudulent transactions	7	1	4	2

RISK SUMMARY CHART

Major Subsystem   INVENTORY

Functional Cell   INPUT

Threat Category	System Vulnerability Description	Harmful Event Description	Index #	Event Prob # Occ/Yr (Rating)	Impact $ Cost/Occ (Rating)	Risk Level (ALE) (Rating)
Malice	Normal batch input process: Vulnerable to unauthorized transaction entry or removal or changes	Resource consuming errors and processing delays	8	2	1	1
	Remote terminals vulnerable to unauthorized use by persons from other work areas or while unstaffed	Resource consuming errors and processing delay	9	2	1	1
	Equipment at unstaffed remote processing areas vulnerable to physical destruction	Fire damage to remote station	10	.12	$64K	$7680
		Water damage to remote station	11	.1	$25K	$2500
		Physical damage to remote station	12	.25	$500	$125

RISK SUMMARY CHART

Major Subsystem <u>INVENTORY</u>

Functional Cell <u>INPUT</u>

Threat Category	System Vulnerability Description	Harmful Event Description	Index #	Event Prob # Occ/Yr (Rating)	Impact $ Cost/Occ (Rating)	Risk Level (ALE) (Rating)
Theft	Equipment at unstaffed remote stations vulnerable to theft	Theft of terminals, modems, supplies	13	1	$140	$1400
		Theft of working papers	14	1	2	1

183

RISK SUMMARY CHART

Major Subsystem   INVENTORY

Functional Cell   INPUT

Threat Category	System Vulnerability Description	Harmful Event Description	Index #	Event Prob # Occ/Yr (Rating)	Impact $ Cost/Occ (Rating)	Risk Level (ALE) (Rating)
Human error	Keystroke errors in batch inputs	Generation of inventory discrepancies requiring manual error diagnosis and recovery	15	1300	$35	$45,500
	Loss or duplication of transactions during input preparation	Generation of inventory discrepancies requiring manual error diagnosis and recovery	16	6	$875	$5250
	Spillage of food and drinks on processing equipment	Damage to terminals or modems	17	1.3	$600	$780

RISK SUMMARY CHART

Major Subsystem   INVENTORY

Functional Cell   INPUT

Threat Category	System Vulnerability Description	Harmful Event Description	Index #	Event Prob # Occ/Yr (Rating)	Impact $ Cost/Occ (Rating)	Risk Level (ALE) (Rating)
Equipment Failure	Remote input stations have no short term backup capability	Equipment failure causing processing delays with required overtime and delayed shipments	18	6	260	$1560

RISK SUMMARY CHART

Major Subsystem: INVENTORY

Functional Cell: INPUT

Threat Category	System Vulnerability Description	Harmful Event Description	Index #	Event Prob # Occ/Yr (Rating)	Impact $ Cost/Occ (Rating)	Risk Level (ALE) (Rating)
Natural Hazards Fire	Several input stations are in warehouse locations with limited fire protection	Fire in an area processing station destroying facility	19	.2	$300	$60
Water	Overhead Sprinklers in some processing stations with no equipment protection	Water damage to equipment and supplies	20	.2	$35,000	$7000

RISK ESTIMATE DETAIL SHEET

INDEX #1

HARMFUL EVENT EXPLANATION:

Unauthorized inputs to the inventory system could be made by people with physical access to any of the remote terminal stations by placing fraudulent transactions into the normal transaction set. This could happen before worksheets are keystroked or during the keystroke process. When punch cards are used, fraudulent cards could be dropped into trays of normal transactions any time before entry into the card reader. Such transactions could conceal the physical theft of items from the warehouses by adjusting inventory levels.

EVENT PROBABILITY ESTIMATE: Rating = 2 (LOW)

Likelihood of occurrence is low since a penetrator would have to know the system operation reasonably well and would derive limited benefit from successful penetration.

IMPACT ESTIMATE: Rating = 2 (LOW)

Impact estimate is low since only limited numbers of fraudulent transactions could be entered without discovery. Also, physical access to the warehouse area is controlled by guard staff.

RISK ESTIMATE DETAIL SHEET

INDEX #2

HARMFUL EVENT EXPLANATION:

(See Index #1)

"Between the lines" transaction could be used to initiate unauthorized shipments of inventory.

EVENT PROBABILITY ESTIMATE: Rating = 2 (LOW)

Likelihood is rated low. Penetrator would require a fair amount of sophistication and frequent access to normal input queries.

IMPACT ESTIMATE: Rating = 4 (HIGH)

Impact is high. If an illegal operation of this type were established, extensive losses could occur over a long period of time.

RISK ESTIMATE DETAIL SHEET

INDEX #3

HARMFUL EVENT EXPLANATION:

Remote terminals in all areas have the same functional capability. A user who would be noticed in his own area if making unauthorized entries, could use a terminal in another functional area without being questioned. When terminals in one area are down, it is customary for users to go to another station to do priority processing. Transactions could conceal *physical theft from inventory*.

EVENT PROBABILITY ESTIMATE: Rating = 3 (MEDIUM)

Likelihood is medium. Any regular system user (there are about 60) or even an unauthorized person would encounter little difficulty accessing terminals in other work areas.

IMPACT ESTIMATE: Rating = 3 (MEDIUM)

Impact estimate is medium. A considerable volume of transaction could be entered in this way and conceal a systematic theft operation.

RISK ESTIMATE DETAIL SHEET

INDEX #4

HARMFUL EVENT EXPLANATION:

(See Index #3)

Fraudulent entries could conceal *unauthorized shipment* of inventory.

EVENT PROBABILITY ESTIMATE: Rating = 3 (MEDIUM)

(See Index #3)

IMPACT ESTIMATE: Rating = 4 (HIGH)

Impact could be quite high since large shipments could be made on a continuing basis.

RISK ESTIMATE DETAIL SHEET

INDEX #5

HARMFUL EVENT EXPLANATION:

All terminals are connected to the system Front End Processor via unprotected private lines communications. Unauthorized terminals could be attached to existing phone lines and used to enter fraudulent transactions to conceal theft or initiate illegal shipments.

EVENT PROBABILITY ESTIMATE: Rating = 3 (MEDIUM)

With a clandestine terminal attached, a penetrator would have opportunity to make extensive fraudulent entries.

IMPACT ESTIMATE: Rating = 4 (HIGH)

Impact estimate is high since extensive operations could be carried on and concealed.

RISK ESTIMATE DETAIL SHEET

INDEX #6

HARMFUL EVENT EXPLANATION:

Terminals in most processing areas are left unattended during off-shifts. These can be activated by a normal sign-on and password entry. They could be used to enter fraudulent transactions that would conceal thefts or initiate illegal shipments.

EVENT PROBABILITY ESTIMATE: Rating = 3 (MEDIUM)

Likelihood seen as medium since preventive security is very low.

IMPACT ESTIMATE: Rating = 4 (HIGH)

Impact estimated as high. (See Index #5)

RISK ESTIMATE DETAIL SHEET

INDEX #7

HARMFUL EVENT EXPLANATION:

Large numbers of people have access to batch transactions and remote terminals. Transactions are not personally accounted. Operations personnel could be persuaded by outsiders to cooperate in collusion to commit fraud.

EVENT PROBABILITY ESTIMATE: Rating = 1 (VERY LOW)

Estimated as very low. Risk to penetrators and the need for cooperation from operation staff reduces vulnerability.

IMPACT ESTIMATE: Rating = 4 (HIGH)

(See Index #5)

RISK ESTIMATE DETAIL SHEET

INDEX #8

HARMFUL EVENT EXPLANATION:

Normal batch inputs could be maliciously disrupted by unauthorized removal of transactions or unauthorized entry of illegitimate transactions.

EVENT PROBABILITY ESTIMATE: Rating = 2 (LOW)

IMPACT ESTIMATE: Rating = 1 (VERY LOW)

Impact would be felt as time consuming errors requiring diagnostic and recovery actions. Errors would be detected during normal inventory surveys.

RISK ESTIMATE DETAIL SHEET

INDEX #9

HARMFUL EVENT EXPLANATION:

(See Index #3)

Remote terminals are vulnerable to unauthorized use by persons from other work areas or while unstaffed. Malicious entry of erroneous transactions could cause resource consuming errors and processing delays.

EVENT PROBABILITY ESTIMATE: Rating = 2 (LOW)

IMPACT ESTIMATE: Rating = 1 (VERY LOW)

RISK ESTIMATE DETAIL SHEET

INDEX #10

HARMFUL EVENT EXPLANATION:

Remote input stations are vulnerable to malicious damage by fire.

EVENT PROBABILITY ESTIMATE: Rating = .12 occ/yr.

Estimate is low based on past experience. There has been one case of known arson affecting an input/output station in 8 years.

IMPACT ESTIMATE: $64,000

Loss of equipment at an RJE station plus cost to recover is about $64,000.

RISK ESTIMATE DETAIL SHEET

INDEX #11

HARMFUL EVENT EXPLANATION:

Some I/O stations are in functional areas protected by sprinklers. Sprinklers could be maliciously activated to damage processing equipment.

EVENT PROBABILITY ESTIMATE: Rating = .1 occ/yr.

IMPACT ESTIMATE: Rating = $25,000

RISK ESTIMATE DETAIL SHEET

INDEX #12

HARMFUL EVENT EXPLANATION:

Many remote stations are in areas vulnerable to vandalism. Physical access to the grounds is limited by normal security force but is easily circumvented. Vandals could damage equipment or communication facilities.

EVENT PROBABILITY ESTIMATE: Rating = .25 occ/yr.

IMPACT ESTIMATE: Rating = $500

Actual acts resulted in an average $500 damage.

RISK ESTIMATE DETAIL SHEET

INDEX #13

HARMFUL EVENT EXPLANATION:

Access to remote station is not well controlled. Processing equipment could be stolen.

EVENT PROBABILITY ESTIMATE: Rating = .10 occ/yr.

Rating is low. Property pass is required to remove equipment from grounds.

IMPACT ESTIMATE: Rating = $1400

Only small pieces of equipment could be removed from grounds without being noticed. Loss of equipment of this sort would average $1400.

RISK ESTIMATE DETAIL SHEET

INDEX #14

HARMFUL EVENT EXPLANATION:

Working papers or official documents could be stolen from the functional areas in which they are used or from areas where keystroking is done.

EVENT PROBABILITY ESTIMATE: Rating = 1 (VERY LOW)

Such documents would be of little value to penetrators.

IMPACT ESTIMATE: Rating = 2 (LOW)

Stolen papers could be reconstructed at low costs.

RISK ESTIMATE DETAIL SHEET

INDEX #15

HARMFUL EVENT EXPLANATION:

Keystroke errors in normal input processing cause record errors, delayed shipments, and time consuming recovery. Physical inventory counts are sometimes needed to validate inventory records.

EVENT PROBABILITY ESTIMATE: Rating = 1300 occ/yr.

Error rate for input transaction is about 5 per day. Keystroke records are verified and edited for valid type, etc., but the 5 errors per day rate continues.

IMPACT ESTIMATE: Rating = $35

Average cost to recover is about $35 per error.

RISK ESTIMATE DETAIL SHEET

INDEX #16

HARMFUL EVENT EXPLANATION:

Portions of input batches occasionally get missed or processed twice. This causes expensive diagnosis and recovery to become necessary.

EVENT PROBABILITY ESTIMATE: Rating = 6 occ/yr.

IMPACT ESTIMATE: Rating = $875

Average cost to recover is about $35 per transaction. Average number of erroneous transactions per event is 25.

RISK ESTIMATE DETAIL SHEET

INDEX #17

HARMFUL EVENT EXPLANATION:

Remote stations are directly in the working areas, and employees are not restricted from heavy food and drinks in these areas. Occasionally things are spilled on equipment, especially terminal keyboards.

EVENT PROBABILITY ESTIMATE: Rating = 1.3 occ/yr.

IMPACT ESTIMATE: Rating = $600

RISK ESTIMATE DETAIL SHEET

INDEX #18

HARMFUL EVENT EXPLANATION:

Remote station equipment failure causes delays in processing. This often results in overtime work.

EVENT PROBABILITY ESTIMATE: Rating = 6 occ/yr.

IMPACT ESTIMATE: Rating = $260

RISK ESTIMATE DETAIL SHEET

INDEX #19

HARMFUL EVENT EXPLANATION:

The shipping and receiving area terminals are located directly in the warehouses. There is no form of fire suppression system in these areas. Possibility of fire in electrical equipment or warehouse mechanical equipment is substantial.

EVENT PROBABILITY ESTIMATE: Rating = .2 occ/yr.

IMPACT ESTIMATE: Rating = $300

Most fires would be discovered and suppressed with type A.B.C. fire extinguishers before damage could take place.

RISK ESTIMATE DETAIL SHEET

INDEX #20

HARMFUL EVENT EXPLANATION:

Overhead sprinklers are found in the personnel and finance and the inventory control areas. These are on circuits protecting fairly large office areas. They are triggered by heat sensors. Water damage to terminal equipment could result even if fire were contained in adjacent areas.

EVENT PROBABILITY ESTIMATE: Rating = .2 occ/yr.

The sprinkler system was installed in 1975 and no incidents have occurred. Rating is an intuitive estimate.

IMPACT ESTIMATE: Rating = $35,000

Major Subsystem: Personnel/Payroll

Functional Cell: Process

Function Description:

The personnel and payroll systems are centrally developed packages that have been slightly modified at Golden State to accommodate local needs. Additionally, several locally written programs access the personnel database to generate reports.

A production program "library" is maintained, and all programmers copy production versions of their programs to the library file when testing is completed. A manual log of additions and changes to the library is kept by the production program librarian.

Access to all personnel and payroll subsystem is controlled by checking of user password at sign-on for on-line programs and at job step initiation for batch programs. The passwords are changed by the program librarian using a special utility program. Access to the password file is controlled by file level access keys.

RISK SUMMARY CHART

Major Subsystem   PERSONNEL/PAYROLL

Functional Cell   PROCESS

Threat Category	System Vulnerability Description	Harmful Event Description	Index #	Event Prob # Occ/Yr (Rating)	Impact $ Cost/Occ (Rating)	Risk Level (ALE) (Rating)
Theft	Proprietary and licensed software easily accessible to any user	Theft of programs from unauthorized source listings or dial-up terminals	21	3	1	2

RISK SUMMARY CHART

Major Subsystem   PERSONNEL

Functional Cell   PROCESS

Threat Category	System Vulnerability Description	Harmful Event Description	Index #	Event Prob # Occ/Yr (Rating)	Impact $ Cost/Occ (Rating)	Risk Level (ALE) (Rating)
Fraud	(cont.)	Changes to systematically modify payroll or personnel data	28	2	3	3
	Operating system is vulnerable to manipulation by assigned systems programmers and other personnel with physical access	O.S. changes to disable file level access protection features	29	3	3	3

RISK SUMMARY CHART

Major Subsystem INVENTORY

Functional Cell INPUT

Threat Category	System Vulnerability Description	Harmful Event Description	Index #	Event Prob # Occ/Yr (Rating)	Impact $ Cost/Occ (Rating)	Risk Level (ALE) (Rating)
Fraud	Applications programs have unlimited data access within a file	Penetrator could circumvent the system access licensing mechanism by writing unauthorized programs	22	3	1	2
	Passwords are maintained on a file with file level security and no protective transforms	Program with password keys can print out the password tables	23	3	5	4
	Console operator can display any memory location contents on system console and system generation link edit is not controlled	Password tables could appear on a system memory dump and be compromised	24	2	5	4
	Production application program library is accessible to all programmers and anyone with file names and access keys	Password tables and protected data are accessed by system operator	25	2	5	4
		Changes to production program to install unauthorized "Trojan Horse" code	26	3	4	4
		Changes to disable edits or production features	27	3	4	4

RISK SUMMARY CHART

Major Subsystem   PERSONNEL

Functional Cell   PROCESS

Threat Category	System Vulnerability Description	Harmful Event Description	Index #	Event Prob # Occ/Yr (Rating)	Impact $ Cost/Occ (Rating)	Risk Level (ALE) (Rating)
Malice	Program library vulnerable to malicious disruption	Disruption of programs, causing errors and delays	30	3	3	3
	Unauthorized physical access to computer facilities possible on some shifts	Malicious destruction of processing equipment	31	2	4	3
	Power supply and environmental support are in an unsecured area	Malicious destruction of support equipment	32	2	4	3
	Main computer room has a back entrance which can be opened only from inside. Door is not visible from most parts of the computer room	Insider could remove material through the rear door or open it to permit unauthorized people to enter	33	3	3	3

211

RISK ESTIMATE DETAIL SHEET

INDEX #21

HARMFUL EVENT EXPLANATION:

A number of vendor supplied proprietary programs and in-house proprietary programs are maintained on the system library and are accessible to most users. Source code could be listed on central site or remote site printers and removed by unauthorized people.

EVENT PROBABILITY ESTIMATE: Rating = 3 (MEDIUM)

No preventive security is evident.

IMPACT ESTIMATE: Rating = 1 (LOW)

Little monetary loss would be incurred, but rapport with vendors and central software development groups would be damaged.

RISK ESTIMATE DETAIL SHEET

INDEX #22

HARMFUL EVENT EXPLANATION:

Access to data files is generally restricted at the file level by operating system access keys. Access to data within a single file is controlled by applications program: an application program can access all of any file for which the keys are known. An application program could be written to allow user access to entire files even when the user is not cleared for some data elements.

EVENT PROBABILITY ESTIMATE: Rating = 3 (MEDIUM)

IMPACT ESTIMATE: Rating = 1 (LOW)

Impact would be low since few files are internally partitioned into elements with different access limits.

RISK ESTIMATE DETAIL SHEET

INDEX #23

HARMFUL EVENT EXPLANATION:

Password tables used to limit user access to terminals are maintained on a system file with locks but no other protection. A penetrator who discovered the file keys could print all passwords in the table.

EVENT PROBABILITY ESTIMATE: Rating = 3 (MEDIUM)

Limited numbers of people have access to the password file keys but risk compromise is substantial.

IMPACT ESTIMATE: Rating = 5 (CRITICAL)

Successful penetration of password tables could expose many of the most important systems including payroll processing.

RISK ESTIMATE DETAIL SHEET

INDEX #24

HARMFUL EVENT EXPLANATION:

System password tables occasionally appear on system memory dumps. The personnel/payroll system password tables are similarly exposed. Hardcopy memory dumps are not well controlled while being printed, stored, and used. Password table could be compromised.

EVENT PROBABILITY ESTIMATE: Rating = 2 (LOW)

IMPACT ESTIMATE: Rating = 5 (CRITICAL)

(See Index #23)

RISK ESTIMATE DETAIL SHEET

INDEX #25

HARMFUL EVENT EXPLANATION:

Console operator can display any memory location contents. Access to printed cross-reference tables showing memory location to tables including passwords is not controlled. A knowledgeable operator could access all user passwords and be able to manipulate personnel or payroll data.

EVENT PROBABILITY ESTIMATE: Rating = 2 (LOW)

IMPACT ESTIMATE: Rating = 5 (CRITICAL)

Compromise of passwords is the most serious effect. Operators would have limited ability to affect stored data.

RISK ESTIMATE DETAIL SHEET

INDEX #26

HARMFUL EVENT EXPLANATION:

Changes could be placed in the source code of production programs, or unauthorized programs could be placed on the executable library to perform fraudulent actions upon request by a penetrator.

EVENT PROBABILITY ESTIMATE: Rating = 3 (MEDIUM)

There is so little preventive security that a relatively unsophisticated fraud could be successful.

IMPACT ESTIMATE: Rating = 4 (HIGH)

Effect could be costly (fraudulent payroll actions) and could be damaging to morale of employees (disclosure of personal data).

RISK ESTIMATE DETAIL SHEET

INDEX #27

HARMFUL EVENT EXPLANATION:

Changes could be made to disable edits on transactions or to disable password protection.

EVENT PROBABILITY ESTIMATE: Rating = 3 (MEDIUM)

(See Index #26)

IMPACT ESTIMATE: Rating = 4 (HIGH)

(See Index #26)

RISK ESTIMATE DETAIL SHEET

INDEX #28

HARMFUL EVENT EXPLANATION:

Programs could be modified to systematically perform fraudulent actions such as adding to an individual's overtime pay or suppressing reporting of adverse personnel actions.

EVENT PROBABILITY ESTIMATE: Rating = 2 (LOW)

The current practice of using multiple programmers on any given applications program maintenance requires collusion of penetrators and reduces opportunity relative to Index #27.

IMPACT ESTIMATE: Rating = 3 (MEDIUM)

RISK ESTIMATE DETAIL SHEET

INDEX #29

HARMFUL EVENT EXPLANATION:

Operating system source code is maintained in files (deck and tape) protected only by file access keys. Many people have access to these files. Changes could be implanted to disable O.S. access protection features.

EVENT PROBABILITY ESTIMATE: Rating = 3 (MEDIUM)

Opportunity is high but value to penetrator is limited since applications systems have their own built-in access limiting features.

IMPACT ESTIMATE: Rating = 3 (MEDIUM)

RISK ESTIMATE DETAIL SHEET

INDEX #30

HARMFUL EVENT EXPLANATION:

Program libraries are accessible (see 29 and 26). Programs could be intentionally modified to cause software failure.

EVENT PROBABILITY ESTIMATE: Rating = 3 (MEDIUM)

Disgruntled employees would find this an easy vulnerability and could inflict damage without being discovered.

IMPACT ESTIMATE: Rating = 3 (MEDIUM)

Recovery from event occurrence could be quite costly.

RISK ESTIMATE DETAIL SHEET

INDEX #31

HARMFUL EVENT EXPLANATION:

Central site equipment could be damaged by unauthorized personnel entering computer room or adjacent area during off-shifts. During regular shifts, unauthorized access to central computer room could be accomplished by waiting at the door until someone walks out, leaving door open momentarily.

EVENT PROBABILITY ESTIMATE: Rating = 2 (LOW)

No such incidents have occurred in the company to date.

IMPACT ESTIMATE: Rating = 4 (HIGH)

Large amounts of damage could be inflicted in terms of equipment losses and delay of processing.

RISK ESTIMATE DETAIL SHEET

INDEX #32

HARMFUL EVENT EXPLANATION:

Destruction of transformers and air conditioning equipment could be accomplished quite easily. This support equipment is in an equipment room at the rear of the administration building.

EVENT PROBABILITY ESTIMATE: Rating = 2 (LOW)

No such incidents have happened to date but preventive security is very low.

IMPACT ESTIMATE: Rating = 4 (HIGH)

Extensive equipment damage and long processing delays would result from occurrence.

RISK ESTIMATE DETAIL SHEET

INDEX #33

HARMFUL EVENT EXPLANATION:

Main computer room has a back entrance which is hidden from most of the room and can be opened from the inside only. An insider could remove material (documents, media, equipment, or maintenance tools) from the room without detection.

EVENT PROBABILITY ESTIMATE: Rating = 3 (MEDIUM)

A number of people have computer room access including operators, maintenance, and custodial personnel.

IMPACT ESTIMATE: Rating = 3 (MEDIUM)

Consolidated Bibliography on EDP Systems Security

Abrams, Marshall, et al., *Tutorial on Computer Security and Integrity*, IEEE Computer Society, Long Beach, CA, 1977.

AFIPS, *Security: Checklist for Computer Center Self-Audits*, AFIPS Press, Washington, DC, 1979.

AFIPS System Review Manual on Security, AFIPS Press, Montvale, NJ, 1974.

Allen, Brandt, "Embezzler's Guide to the Computer," pp. 79–89, *Harvard Business Review*, July–August 1975.

Attanasio, C. R., Markstein, P. W., and Phillips, R. J., "Penetrating an Operating System: A Study of VM/370 Integrity," *IBM Systems Journal*, Volume 15, Number 1, pp. 102–116, 1976.

Blanc, Robert P., Ed., *An Analysis of Computer Security Safeguards for Detecting and Preventing Intentional Computer Misuse*, National Bureau of Standards Special Publication 500-25, 1978.

Brandstad, Dennis K., Ed., *Computer Security and the Data Encryption Standard*, National Bureau of Standards Special Publication 500-27, 1978.

Campbell, Robert, et al., Army Regulation 380-380, "Automated Systems Security," 1977.

Conway, R. W., Maxwell, W. L., and Morgan, H. L., "On the Implementation of Security Measures in Automation Systems," *Communications of the ACM*, Volume 15, Number 4, April 1972.

Date, C. J., *An Introduction To Data Base Systems*, Addison-Wesley Publishing Co., Reading, MA, 1976.

Department of Defense Manual 5220.22-M, "Industrial Security Manual for Safeguarding Classified Information," 1977.

Dinardo, C. T., *Computers and Security*, Information Technology Series Vol. III, AFIPS Press, Montvale, NJ, 1978.

Donovan, J. J., and Madnick, S. E., "Hierarchical Approach to Computer System Integrity," *IBM Systems Journal*, Volume 14, Number 2, pp. 188–202, 1975.

Fitzgerald, Jerry, *Internal Controls for Computerized Systems*, E. M. Underwood, San Leandro, CA 1978.

Hoffman, Lance J., *Modern Methods for Computer Security and Privacy*, Prentice-Hall, Englewood Cliffs, NJ, 1977.

Hoffman, Lance J., et al., "SECURATE—Security Evaluation and Analysis Using Fuzzy Metrics," pp. 531–538, *Journal of National Computer Conference*, 1978.

Hsiao, David; Kerr, Douglas; and Madnick, S. E., *Computer Security*, Academic Press, New York, NY, 1979.

IBM, "The Considerations of Physical Security in a Computer Environment," G520-2700-0, 1972.

IBM, "Customer Information Control System/Virtual Storage (CICS/VS) General Information Manual," GH20-1280-4, 1975.

IBM, "Data Security Controls and Procedures—A Philosophy for DP Installations," G320-5049-1, 1977.

IBM, "IMS/VS Data Base Recovery Control Feature General Information," GH35-0010-1, 1979.

IBM, "IMS/VS Version 1 General Information Manual," GT00-0442-0, 1977.

IBM, "OS/VS2 MVS Utilities," GC26-3902-0, 1977.

Jacobson, Robert V., et al., *Guidelines for Automatic Data Processing Physical Security and Risk Management*, Federal Information Processing Standards Publication 31, National Bureau of Standards, 1974.

Jancura, Elise J., and Berger, Arnold H., *Computers: Auditing and Control*, Auerbach, Philadelphia, PA, 1973.

Kapp, Dan, and Leben, Joseph F., *IMS Programming Techniques*, Van Nostrand Reinhold, New York, NY, 1978.

Krause, L. I., and MacGahan, A., *Computer Fraud and Countermeasures*, Prentice-Hall, Englewood Cliffs, NJ, 1979.

Lord, Keniston W., Jr., *The Data Center Disaster Consultant*, QED, Wellesley, MA, 1977.

Martin, James, *Computer Data Base Organization*, Prentice-Hall, Englewood Cliffs, NJ, 1975.

National Criminal Justice Information and Statistics Service, *Computer Crime: Criminal Justice Resource Manual*, Dept. of Justice, Stock Number 027-000-00870-4, 1979.

National Technical Information Service, *Countermeasures*, AD-A072-245, Dept. of Commerce, Springfield, VA, 1979.

National Technical Information Service, *Risk Analysis Methodology*, AD-A072-249, Dept. of Commerce, Springfield, VA, 1979.

Martin, James, *Principles of Data Base Management*, Prentice-Hall, Englewood Cliffs, NJ, 1976.

Martin, James, *Security, Accuracy, and Privacy in Computer Systems*, Prentice-Hall, Englewood Cliffs, NJ, 1973.

Nielson, N. R., et al., *Computer System Integrity, A Relative-Impact Measure of Vulnerability*, Stanford Research Institute, Menlo Park, CA, 1978.

Personal Privacy in an Information Society, the Report of the Privacy Protection Study Commission, U.S. Government Printing Office, 1978.

Reed, Susan K., *Automatic Data Processing Risk Assessment*, National Bureau of Standards NBSIR 77-1228, 1977.

Ruthberg, Zella, and McKenzie, Robert G., *Audit and Evaluation of Computer Security*, National Bureau of Standards Special Publication 500-19, 1977.

Shaw, Alan C., *The Logical Design of Operating Systems*, Prentice-Hall, Englewood Cliffs, NJ, 1974.

Troy, Eugene F., et al., Army Regulation 18-7, "Data Processing Activity Management, Procedures, and Standards," 1978.

U.S. Senate, Committee on Government Operations, "Staff Study of Computer Security in Federal Programs," 1977.

Van Tassel, Dennis, *Computer Security Management*, Prentice-Hall, Englewood Cliffs, NJ, 1972.

Wood, Helen M., *The Use of Passwords for Controlled Access to Computer Resources*, National Bureau of Standards Special Publication 500-9, 1977.

Whiteside, Thomas, *Computer Capers*, Thomas V. Crowell Co., NY, 1978.

Bibliography

Bloombecker, Bock, *Spectacular Computer Crimes*, Dow Jones-Irwin, Homewood, IL, 1990.

Burger, Ralf, *Computer Viruses: A High-Tech Disease*, Abacus, Grand Rapids, MI, 1988.

Day, Chet, *The Hacker*, Pocket Books, New York, NY, 1989.

Dvorak, John C., *PC Crash Course and Survival Guide*, Scandanavian P.C. Systems, 1990

Goldstein, Larry Joel, *IBM PC and Compatibles*, 4th. ed., Prentice-Hall, Englewood Cliffs, NJ, 1989.

Haynes, Colin, *The Computer Virus Protection Handbook*, SYBEX, San Francisco, CA, 1990.

Juliussen, Karen and Egil, *The Computer Industry Almanac 1990*, Brady, New York, NY, 1990.

Krumm, Robert, *Getting the Most from Utilities on the IBM PC*, Brady, New York, NY, 1986.

Levin, Richard B., *The Computer Virus Handbook*, McGraw-Hill, Berkeley, CA, 1990.

Lv, Cary, *The Apple Macintosh Book*, 3rd. ed., Microsoft Press, Redmond, WA, 1985.

Mace, Paul, *The Paul Mace Guide to Data Processing*, Brady, New York, NY, 1988.

Mair, W., Wood, Donald, and Davis, K. W., *Computer Control & Audit*, QED Information Sciences, Wellesley, MA, 1978.

Martin, James, *Information Engineering Book I: Introduction*, Prentice-Hall, Englewood Cliffs, NJ, 1989.

Martin, James, *An Information Systems Manifesto*, Prentice-Hall, Englewood Cliffs, NJ, 1984.

Martin, James, *Information Engineering Book II: Planning & Analysis*, Prentice-Hall, Englewood Cliffs, NJ, 1990.

Mayo, Jonathan L., *Computer Viruses: What They Are, How They Work, and How to Avoid Them*, Windcrest, Blue Ridge Summit, PA, 1989 (includes anti-viral shareware disk).

McWilliams, Peter, *The Personal Computer Book*, Prelude Press, Los Angeles, CA, 1990.

Morris, Robert, *DOS, WordPerfect & LOTUS, Office Companion*, Ventana Press, Chapel Hill, NC, 1990.

Murray, Katherine, *Introduction to Personal Computing*, Que Corp., Carmel, IN, 1990.

Norton, Peter, and Wilton, Richard, *The IBM PC & PS/2 Programmers Guide*, Microsoft Press, Redmond, WA, 1988.

Norton, Peter, *Inside the IBM PC*, Brady Book, New York, NY, 1986; Que Corp., Carmel, IN, 1989.

Perry, William E., *Handbook of Diagnosing and Solving Computer Problems*, TAB Books, 1989.

Rubin, Charles, *Microsoft Works for the Apple Macintosh*, Microsoft Press, Redmond, WA, 1989.

Sawusch, Mark R., *The Best of Shareware*, Wingcrest, Blue Ridge Summit, PA, 1990 (includes disk of utilities).

Shore, Joel, *Using Computers in Business*, Que Corp., Carmel, IN, 1989.

Stoll, Clifford, *The Cuckoo's Egg*, Doubleday, Garden City, NY, 1989.

Toigo, Jon William, *Disaster Recovery Planning: Managing Risk & Catastrophe in Information Systems*, Yourdon Press, Englewood Cliffs, NJ, 1989.

Turley, James L., *PCs Made Easy*, McGraw-Hill, Berkeley, CA, 1989.

Vitus, Bob, *Dr. Macintosh, Tips, Techniques, and Advice on Mastering the Macintosh*, Addison-Wesley, Reading, MA, 1989.

Wang, W. E. and Kraynak, Joe, *First Book of Personal Computing*, Macmillan, Inc., New York, NY 1990.

Glossary of Terms Used in EDP System Security

access

Gaining admittance to data in any manner, or making use of any resources in a computer system. It specifically refers to a set of protective counter-measures against unauthorized admittance to, or disclosure of, data.

access authorization

Permission granted to an object (person, terminal, program) to perform a set of operations in the system. Access authorization is commonly expressed in terms of a profile matrix which gives access privileges in terms of users, terminals, programs, data elements, type of access (e.g., read, write), and time period when operations are permitted.

application disaster recovery plan

The plan developed to process an application after it has been disrupted for some period of time.

audit trail

A chronological record of system activities which is sufficient to enable the reconstruction, review, and examination of the sequence of environments and activities surrounding or leading to each event in the path of a transaction from its inception to output of final results. Note: This is the industry accepted standard term.

backup and recovery procedures

The provisions made for the recovery of data files and program libraries, and for restart or replacement of EDP equipment after system failure or a disaster.

bounds checking
Testing of computer program results for access to storage outside of its authorized limits. Synonymous with memory bounds checking.

bounds register
A hardware register which holds an address specifying a storage boundary.

browsing
Searching through storage to locate or acquire information, without necessarily knowing of the existence or the format of the information being sought.

call back
A procedure established for identifying a terminal dialing into a computer system by disconnecting the calling terminal and re-establishing the connection with the computer system dialing the telephone number of the calling terminal.

compartmentalization
(a) The isolation of the operating system, user programs, and data files from one another in main storage in order to provide protection against unauthorized or concurrent access by other users or programs.
(b) The breaking down of sensitive data into small, isolated blocks for the purpose of reducing risk to the data.

complete mediation of accesses
Checking all attempts to access the system or data for levels of authorization privilege before access is granted.

compromising emanations
Data-related signals transmitted as radiation through the air and through conductors. If intercepted and analyzed, they could disclose information being transmitted, received, or processed by any information systems equipment.

contingency planning
The process of creating a disaster recovery plan and a contingency program.

contingency program
The day-to-day work activities and procedures, such as backing up critical data files, that fulfill the requirements of recoverability.

controls
Methods used to regulate the system so that it performs according to specified criteria. Generally identical to **countermeasures**.

cost-benefit analysis
The assessment of the costs of potential risk of loss or compromise of data in an EDP system without data protection versus the cost of providing data protection.

countermeasures
Methods of any type (e.g., physical, procedural, hardware, software, personnel) employed to counteract a threat to the system.

critical processing
Those applications that have been defined as being so important to the operation of the company that little or no loss of availability is acceptable.

data security
    The protection of data from accidental, unauthorized, intentional, or malicious modification, destruction, or disclosure.

decrypt
    To convert, by use of the appropriate key, encrypted (encoded or enciphered) text into its equivalent plain text. See also **encrypt**.

default to denial of access
    Designing a system so that access authorizations are mandatory and those without the authorization are locked out.

disaster recovery manual
    The documentation of the disaster recovery plan, including a discussion of activities to be performed, with supporting documents and checklists.

disaster recovery operation
    The operation of recovering from the effects of a computer facility disruption, and restoring, in a preplanned manner, the capabilities of the facility.

disaster recovery plan
    The preplanned sequence of events that allows for the recovery of a computer facility and/or the applications processed there.

discretionary processing
    Those applications that may be interrupted for some period of time. A loss of the ability to process these applications for some period of time will not seriously affect the well-being of the company.

economy of mechanism
    Keeping the security design as small and simple as possible. The more complex any system is, the greater the number of potential errors.

EDP system security
    The hardware/software functions, characteristics and features; operational procedures, accountability procedures and access controls at the central computer facility, remote computer, and terminal facilities; the management constraints, physical structure, and devices; and personnel and communications controls needed to provide an acceptable level of protection in a computer system.

encrypt
    To convert plain text into unintelligible form by means of cryptographic system. See also **decrypt**.

entrapment
    The deliberate planting of apparent flaws in a system for the purpose of detecting attempted penetrations.

exposure
    The degree of relative availability of data in the environment in which it is used. In this sense, data exposure is one major aspect of system vulnerability. Access and usage (see also **access** and **usage**) are the two major categories of exposure.

fetch protection
    A system-provided restriction to prevent a program from accessing data in another user's segment of storage.

hardware security
Computer equipment features or devices used in an EDP system to preclude unauthorized access to data or system resources.

harmful event
An instance of a threat acting upon a system vulnerability, in which the system is adversely affected. This may include physical damage to elements of the system or may be manifested in: denial of service, unauthorized use of data or system resources, unauthorized manipulation of data or programs for fraudulent purposes, or unauthorized disclosure of information.

identity authentication
A set of manual or automated procedures which verify that a user requesting access is who he/she claims to be. These include passwords, questions, measurement of physical attributes (e.g., hand geometry), and other mechanisms.

impact
Damage to the organization as a result of a harmful event (threat acting upon a vulnerability of the system). Impact is usually measured in dollars of loss per occurrence, but in more complex circumstances may be measured qualitatively by means of an ordinal scale (low to high) or by comparison. See also **loss**.

impact analysis
The measure of amount of loss from a harmful event.

individual accountability
Measures to positively associate the identity of a user with his access to machines; material; and the time, method, and degree of access.

integrity
(a) The capability of an EDP system to perform its intended function in an unimpaired manner, free from deliberate or inadvertent unauthorized manipulation of the system.
(b) Completeness and accuracy of data, either as separate elements or in consistency of relationship among elements. Includes the concept of continued data existence and recoverability from error.

isolation
See **compartmentalization**.

journaling
An in-depth form of logging, in which all significant access or file activity events are recorded in their entirety. A complete journal would have a record, for example, of all data elements accessed by a user, the old and new images of any data changed, any images added or deleted, and the like. Using earlier copies of a file, plus a journal, it would be possible to reconstruct the file at any point and identify the ways it has changed over a period of time.

least common mechanism
A concept that more than one program or user should not share file work areas because an exploitable data path could result.

least privilege

The granting of the minimum access authorization necessary for the performance of required tasks. Refers to the access profile matrix, in which each user, terminal, program, and type of data element may be given a separate access sensitivity license. For any combination of these factors, the lowest privilege of access of any of the factors will govern the access license for the whole combination.

logging

A record that is kept either manually or by the computer system to keep track of events that take place with respect to the system.

loss

As used in risk management, loss is the quantitative measure of expected deprivation due to a threat acting upon a vulnerable system resource. Annualized Loss Expectancy is the product of the expected loss per harmful event times the probable number of times the harmful event is expected to occur in a year's time.

masquerading

An attempt to gain access to a system by posing as an authorized user.

multiple access rights terminal

A terminal that may be used by more than one class of users; for example, users with different access rights to data.

nonsecret design

Security holes overlooked by the designers which can be found by bright people given free opportunity to examine the system under development. For example, a modern principle of cryptography is that it is expected that the enemy may know how the system works, but is still prohibited from access to the system because he/she cannot obtain the necessary keys or enabling parameters.

objectives of defense

All security defensive measures intended to satisfy one or more of the following objectives:

(a) Prevent occurrence of the exposure by erecting barriers between any threat and the vulnerabilities to it.

(b) Minimize or contain the impact of any damage, mainly through the use of successive layers of protection so that a threat agent is restricted in what it can do.

(c) Maximize recovery from the damage. Provide for ways of circumventing the damage, such as by the use of backup and reconstruction of files.

operational data security

The protection of data from either accidental or unauthorized, intentional modification, destruction, or disclosure during input, processing, or output operations.

overwriting

The obliteration of recorded data by recording different data on the same medium.

password
> A protected word or a string of characters that identifies or authenticates a user, a specific resource, or an access type.

personnel security
> The procedures established to ensure that all personnel who have access to any sensitive information have the required authorities as well as all appropriate clearances.

physical security
> (a) The use of locks, guards, badges, and similar measures to control access to the computer and related equipment.
>
> (b) The measures required for the protection of the structures housing the computer with related equipment and their contents from damage by accident, fire, and environmental hazards.

piggy back entry
> Unauthorized access that is gained to an EDP system via another user's legitimate connection.

privacy
> (a) The right of an individual to self-determination as to the degree to which the individual is willing to share with others information about himself that may be compromised by unauthorized exchange of such information among other individuals or organizations.
>
> (b) The right of individuals and organizations to control the collection, storage, and dissemination of their data or information about themselves.

procedural security
> The management constraints; operational, administrative and accountability procedures; and supplemental controls established to provide an acceptable level of protection for sensitive defense information and data.

protection
> Defense or safeguard against attack by some intentional or unintentional threat agent.

reliability
> Dependability of a system to perform exactly as expected, without error.

remote terminal area
> Remote computer facilities, peripheral devices, or terminals which are located outside the central computer facility.

residue
> Data left in storage after processing operations and before degaussing or re-writing has taken place.

risk
> The probability or likelihood that a threat agent will successfully mount a specific attack against a particular system vulnerability.

risk analysis
> A method of analyzing system assets and vulnerabilities to establish an expected loss from harmful events based upon probabilities of occurrence. The object of risk analysis is to assess the degree of acceptability of each risk to system operation.

risk assessment
The process of evaluating threats and vulnerabilities, both known and postulated, to determine expected loss and establish the degree of acceptability to system operations.

risk management
An element of managerial science concerned with the identification, measurement, control, and minimization of uncertain events. An effective risk management program encompasses the following four phases: (1) Risk Assessment, as derived from an evaluation of threats and vulnerabilities; (2) Management Decision; (3) Control Implementation; and (4) Effectiveness Review.

scavenging
Searching through residue for the purpose of unauthorized data acquisition.

security
(a) The protection of data system resources against accidental or intentional destruction, disclosure, or modification. Computer security refers to technological safeguards and managerial procedures which can be applied to system resources to protect organizational assets and individual privacy. In this book, security is often used to encompass three other important ideas taken together: protection, integrity, and reliability (q.v.).
(b) See also: **data security; EDP system security; personnel security; physical security; procedural security**.

separation of duties or functions
Structuring system-related jobs so that each has as little security exposure as is feasible for efficient operation. For execution of critical tasks, the intervention of more than one person should be required. The general principle is to reduce the opportunity of any one person to subvert or damage the system.

separation of privilege
Requiring access authorization from more than one privileged object for highly sensitive systems or data. As an example, gaining access to the access authorization matrix in order to change levels should require the formal collaboration of two trusted employees, each knowing only part of the procedure or access parameters.

software security
Those general purpose (executive, utility, or software development tools) and applications programs and routines which protect data or information handled by an EDP system and its resources.

system integrity
The state that exists when there is complete assurance that under all conditions an EDP system is based on the logical correctness and reliability of the operating system, the logical completeness of the hardware and software that implement the protection mechanisms, and data integrity.

technological attack

An attack which can be perpetrated by circumventing or nullifying hardware and software access control mechanisms, rather than by subverting system personnel or other users.

threat

An aspect of the systems environment that, if given an opportunity, could cause a harmful event to occur. See also **harmful event** and **vulnerability**.

trap door

A condition existing in the system software or hardware which can be triggered to subvert the software or hardware security features. Basically there are two kinds of trap doors: first, the condition is triggered by something internal to the system (e.g., a counter, a date/time value, or any specific set of preestablished circumstances); second, a condition is triggered by an external input to the system (e.g., a remote terminal or application program input message).

Trojan horse

A computer program that is apparently or actually useful and that contains a trap door.

usage

Relating to the integrity of data, this term specifically refers to a set of protective countermeasures to assure and maintain validity of data and to provide for its continued existence and recoverability.

user

The function or organization that receives and uses the output of a computer application. User functions are outside the physical boundary of the computer facility, but the user may directly interface with the system via a terminal.

used alternative plan

The set of plans for use by the user of an application when the processing of that application has been disrupted. This may consist of: do nothing, manual methods, or a standby processor.

vulnerability

Any weakness or flaw existing in a system. More specifically, the susceptibility of a system to a specific threat attack or harmful event, or the opportunity available to a threat agent to mount that attack. A vulnerability in a system may exist independently of any known threat.

work factor

An estimate of the effort or time that can be expected to be expended to overcome a protective measure by a would-be penetrator with specified expertise and resources.

A Sample Outline for a Corporate Security Manual

INTRODUCTION
Definition of Data Security
Need for Data Security
Security Awareness
Familiarization with Data Security Handbook
Corporate Description of Data Security Department's Role

CORPORATE ISSUES
Ownership of Programs and Data
Legal Considerations
Auditing Considerations
Foreign Corrupt Practices Act
Data Privacy Issues

PERSONNEL CONSIDERATIONS
Employee Obligations to Protect Corporate Assets
Non-disclosure Agreement
Dissemination of Sensitive Data
Lack of Compliance and Disciplinary Actions

ASSESSMENT OF DATA AND APPLICATIONS
Risk Analysis
Classification of Data
Prioritizing Software

ACCIDENTAL DISCLOSURE
Public Display of Passwords
Unattended Terminals

USER AUTHORIZATION
Authentication of Users
Creation and Maintenance of Access Identification Tables
Frequency of Password Update
File Security
Dial-up Security

NAMING STANDARDS
Access IDs
Datasets (Non-IMS)
Passwords
IMS Datasets

PROGRAM LIBRARIES
Production Library Control
Production Library Control Inventory Listings
Change Logs
Version-based Maintenance
Monitoring Changes to Source Code
Emergency Access

DATABASE INTEGRITY
General Statement

IMS-RELATED SECURITY—IMS/VS
General Statement on IMS/VS
Terminal Security
Password Security
Logical Data Structures
Field and Segment-level Sensitivity
Security Maintenance Utility

THIRD-PARTY UTILITY SOFTWARE
Top Secret
Net/Guard

DATA STORAGE
Volume Security
Tape Library Security

PERSONAL COMPUTER SECURITY ISSUES

PC Security Overview
Data Encryption
License Agreements
Storage of Diskettes
Backup Procedures
Micro-Mainframe Connections
Physical Security

ONGOING SURVEILLANCE

Unsuccessful Access Attempts
Presence of Unexplained Code
Unexplained Data Communications Patterns
Unexplained Hardware/Software Failures

POINTS OF DATA EXPOSURE

General Statement regarding Data Gathering, Data Input, Data
Conversion, Data Communication, Data Processing, Data Output,
and Data Preparation

DATA CONTROLS

General Statement regarding Preventative, Detective, and
Corrective Controls; Transmittal Documents; Batch Control
Tickets; Batch Balancing/Hash Controls; Suspense Files; and
Redundancy Processing

Index